AGS

Life Scientists

Reading in the Content Area

AGS®

American Guidance Service, Inc.
4201 Woodland Road
Circle Pines, MN 55014-1796
1-800-328-2560

Carol A. Maccini

Photo credits:

cover—(Jane Goodall, mother and twin chimps, Gombe Game Preserve) National Geographic; pp. 9, 13—Corbis; p. 17—Baldwin H. Ward & Kathryn C. Ward/Corbis; pp. 21, 25, 31—Corbis; p. 35—Hulton Getty Picture Collection; pp. 39, 43, 47, 53—Corbis; p. 57—National Portrait Gallery, Smithsonian Institution; pp. 61, 65—Corbis; p. 69—Evan Kafka/Liaison Agency; p. 75—Hulton Getty Picture Collection; p. 79—Corbis; p. 83—Karl Ammann/Corbis; p. 87—Corbis

Printed in the United States of America

ISBN 0-7854-2425-3

Order Number: 91560

A 0 9 8 7 6 5 4 5 3 2 1

Contents

Note to Students

Life Scientists includes 19 lessons, one on each of 19 scientists. The purpose of the book is twofold: (1) to give you a brief biographical sketch of each scientist and the work that each has done and (2) to acquaint you with a study technique for reading content area material. It interweaves content and process.

Content
The content covers a period from the early 1700s to the present. It gives an overview of important scientific events. It also touches upon characteristics of each scientist and scientific beliefs of the time.

Developing a Sense of Text
Many students who are good story readers have difficulty reading textbooks. Sometimes it is hard to understand or remember what you have read. A story and a textbook selection have different structures.

A story has a familiar structure, or "story line." Usually, it begins with a setting. Next, a character with a problem (or a goal) is introduced. The character then tries to solve the problem. Finally, the problem is resolved, and the story ends.

Structure of the Story Line					
Setting	Character	Problem	Attempts	Resolution	Ending

Textbooks may seem harder to read because they have a less familiar structure. Textbook authors help readers by providing guidelines such as a title, an introduction, headings, a summary, and review questions. These aids help the reader to understand the text.

Structure of the Text Line				
Title	Introduction	Headings	Summary	Questions

This workbook is designed to help you understand how to read textbooks. Each lesson begins with a preview that clearly presents the subject and the structure of the selection. The text itself includes an introduction, headings, and a summary. The lesson ends with a set of questions designed to help you remember and think about what you read.

Learning a Study Technique

The study technique used in this book involves seven steps: Preview, Prepare, Read and Record, Review, Rethink, React and Write, and Experiment. Using these seven steps will help you develop a sense of text.

Preview

The intent of the Preview is to help make you conscious of the subject about which you will be reading. You are asked to use the title and subheadings to complete a map. This should allow you to make an accurate prediction about the content that follows. It is important to have an idea of what to expect when reading any material.

Prepare

The Prepare section offers a second pre-reading activity. You are to prepare for reading by matching vocabulary words with their meanings. If you have trouble with this activity, try these two steps: (1) Find the boldface word in the text and read the sentences surrounding the word. This is called *getting the meaning from context*. (2) Use the glossary to find the meaning of the word.

It can be hard to understand what you are reading if you do not know the individual meanings of the words. As you read, if you find other words you do not know, stop and find their meanings before continuing.

Read and Record

Read through the complete text. You are then asked to place significant dates from the story on a timeline. You will also place dates from previous lessons, your birth date, and other historical dates on the timeline.

Review

You are asked to read the information a second time. As you read, you are asked to complete activities to show an overall understanding of the text. Read one section at a time, and then fill in that part of the activity. Skim quickly to find this information rather than reading word for word.

Review your completed activity. Notice how the pieces of information fit together.

Rethink

In this section you will answer questions using the information you have read. You might find it helpful to scan through the article and reread the information. You may not find exact answers to the questions. You will have to create your own answers by using the given information. This will help you organize and express your thoughts.

React and Write

The React and Write section helps you tie the information you have read to both your base of experiences and the world in which you live.

Having a background for the topics can help you understand what you are reading. You may have seen movies, listened to speeches, or read articles related to the topic. Thinking about these experiences can open your mind to the topic.

Under a Microscope: Getting the Main Idea

In this unit, you will learn about five scientists who spent much of their working lives looking at tiny organisms under a microscope. The willingness of these scientists to work hard means you no longer have to worry about many of the deadly diseases that were so common only a short time ago. These diseases were all caused by tiny organisms that harm people. These scientists were able to discover ways to fight off such organisms.

You will learn about scientists who made your food safe to eat, cured diseases, and discovered new drugs. These scientists had to work hard under personal and professional obstacles to make their discoveries. They were all willing to do so because saving lives was important to them.

While you are reading about these five scientists, consider the main idea in each selection. Just as the scientists never lost sight of the main idea in their research, so must you never lose sight of the main idea when you are reading a textbook.

Textbooks help you follow the main idea by providing hints through introductions, headings, summaries, and sometimes titles. Also, each paragraph often begins with a topic sentence that states the main idea. If that main idea sentence is not actually written in the paragraph, you should still be able to figure it out. All the sentences in a paragraph provide details that point to the main idea of the paragraph.

 When you are finished with this unit, place one significant date for each scientist you learned about on this timeline.

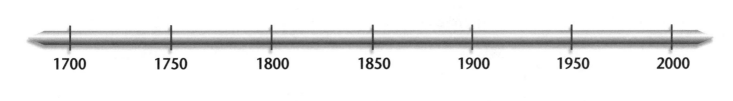

| 1700 | 1750 | 1800 | 1850 | 1900 | 1950 | 2000 |

Edward Jenner   (1749–1823)

Preview: Look through the text. Find the author's subject and main topics. Do this by looking at the title of the article and the boldface headings marked A, B, C, and D. Use this information to predict the main idea of this article.

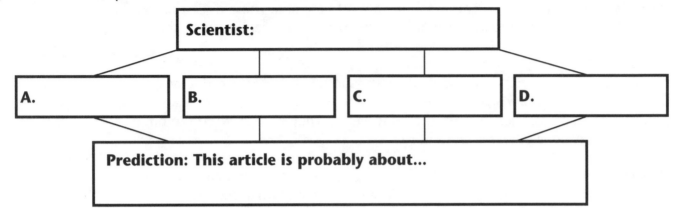

Scientist:

A.

B.

C.

D.

Prediction: This article is probably about...

Prepare: Match each definition with the correct word. Use the glossary if you need help.

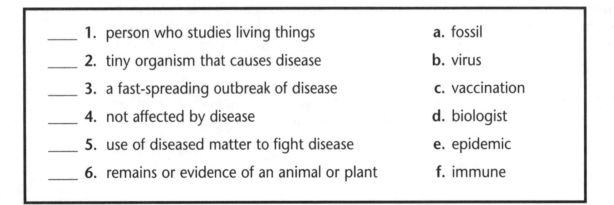

_____ 1. person who studies living things	**a.** fossil
_____ 2. tiny organism that causes disease	**b.** virus
_____ 3. a fast-spreading outbreak of disease	**c.** vaccination
_____ 4. not affected by disease	**d.** biologist
_____ 5. use of diseased matter to fight disease	**e.** epidemic
_____ 6. remains or evidence of an animal or plant	**f.** immune

Edward Jenner

Edward Jenner was a British **biologist**. He was a pioneer in **vaccination** and in the study of the **immune** system. Jenner's work led to the control of the smallpox disease. He invented the word *virus* to describe the tiny organisms that cause this disease.

A. Early Life
Edward Jenner was born on May 17, 1749, in Berkeley, Gloucestershire, England. When he was five, both of his parents died. Edward, the sixth and youngest child, came under the guardianship of his older brother.

Edward was educated in the local schools. He enjoyed searching for **fossils** when he was a boy. A fossil is a rock that shows the imprint of an animal or plant that lived long ago.

In 1761, Jenner went to work for a surgeon, Daniel Ludlow. He studied with Ludlow until 1770. Then, he went to London to study under John Hunter at St. Georges Hospital.

B. Jenner's Discovery

Jenner returned to Gloucestershire to work as an apprentice and, later, as a doctor. Along with practicing medicine, Jenner wrote poetry, played the flute, and wrote articles about nature.

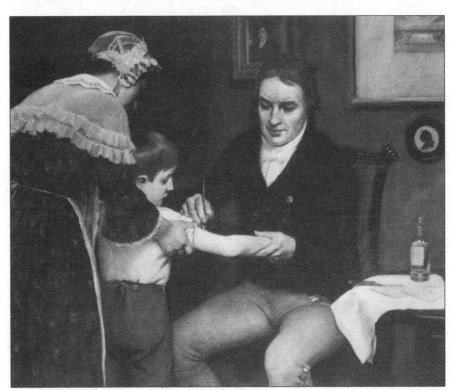

Edward Jenner controlled the spread of smallpox. He was the first doctor to use vaccination to protect against disease.

In 1788, a deadly smallpox **epidemic** broke out in England. The disease was cruel. Victims faced high fever, pimple-like **infections,** and possible death.

A crude **inoculation** was available. First, a doctor would collect matter from a smallpox victim who had a light case of the disease. Then, the patient's vein would be scratched. Finally, the doctor would work some of the infected matter into the vein. Sometimes, the patient would have a mild reaction and then become immune to smallpox. Other times, the patient would get a hard case of smallpox and die. This method was the best way doctors knew of to protect people from smallpox.

Like other doctors, Jenner began doing the crude inoculations. It was the only hope he could offer his patients. Some of his patients did not react to the smallpox. Jenner discovered that those who did not react had once been infected with cowpox. This less serious disease sometimes affected cows and the people who milked them. Jenner realized that people who had once suffered from cowpox never got smallpox.

C. Successful Smallpox Vaccinations

Jenner experimented on this connection between cowpox and smallpox. On May 14, 1796, eight-year-old James Phipps became the first person inoculated against smallpox with Jenner's method.

Jenner injected the boy with a speck of virus from cowpox. Forty-eight days later, he injected the boy with smallpox matter. The cowpox injection protected the boy from getting a serious case of smallpox. The smallpox matter gave the boy's body a way to fight smallpox. The boy became immune to the disease. The process came to be called vaccination, named after *vaccinia,* the medical word for cowpox.

Jenner wanted to present his findings to the Royal Society, a group of important scientists in England. Jenner decided not to approach the group because his findings were different from current beliefs. In 1798, Jenner published his work privately. In his article, he introduced the term *virus* to describe the **microbe** that produced smallpox.

D. Spread of Vaccinations

Jenner continued work on this vaccine for the rest of his life. He discovered that the vaccine would remain usable for three months. Jenner sent it to doctors all over the world. He even sent some of the vaccine to America's President, Thomas Jefferson.

Jenner worked long hours, sometimes vaccinating up to 300 patients in one day. Until his death, Jenner supported the vaccination idea in speeches and papers. Edward Jenner died on January 26, 1823.

Summary

Edward Jenner controlled the spread of smallpox. He also set the stage for the disease to be eliminated from the world within the next 200 years. He was the first to use a virus for **immunization.** Now, cures for many other diseases are based on that same idea. As a result of his research, Jenner was responsible for saving thousands of lives.

Read and Record: Place the following dates on the timeline:

(1) Edward Jenner's birth
(2) Smallpox epidemic in England
(3) First smallpox vaccination
(4) Edward Jenner's death
(5) First U.S. President (1789)
(6) First person on the moon (1969)
(7) Your birth date
(8) First airplane flight (1903)

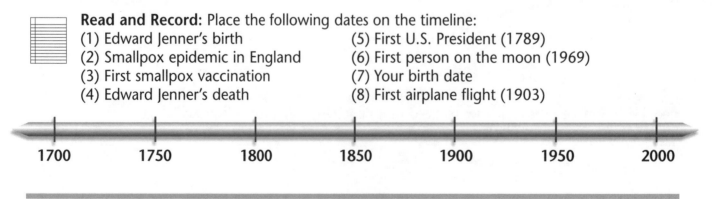

1700   1750   1800   1850   1900   1950   2000

Review: Fill in this Main Idea chart. Write a title that captures the overall meaning of the article. List the four sections of the article and write three main ideas about each section.

	Title			
A.				
B.				
C.				
D.				

 Rethink: Answer each of the following questions.

1. Why did Edward Jenner create the word *virus*?

_____

_____

2. The early, crude inoculations only worked part of the time. Why do you think Dr. Jenner's inoculation worked better?

_____

_____

React and Write: Answer #1 with a complete sentence and #2 with a drawing.

1. During a smallpox outbreak in 1785, a young man said, "I'd rather be a dairy farmer than die." Explain his statement. _____ _____ _____	**2.** Until the 1980s, smallpox vaccinations were routine. Find a relative who has had a smallpox vaccination. Draw a picture of the vaccination.

Louis Pasteur   (1822–1895)

Preview: Look through the text. Find the author's subject and main topics. Do this by looking at the title of the article and the boldface headings marked A, B, C, and D. Use this information to predict the main idea of this article.

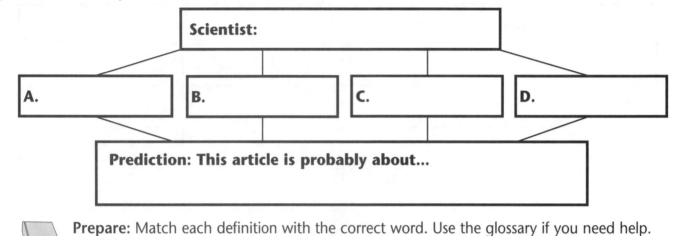

Scientist:

A.   **B.**   **C.**   **D.**

Prediction: This article is probably about...

Prepare: Match each definition with the correct word. Use the glossary if you need help.

_____ 1. person who studies very small life forms   **a.** fermentation

_____ 2. tiny life form   **b.** rabid

_____ 3. chemical reaction used to make wine   **c.** spontaneous generation

_____ 4. process used to keep food germ-free   **d.** microbiologist

_____ 5. life grows from non-living matter   **e.** pasteurization

_____ 6. has rabies   **f.** microbe

Louis Pasteur

Louis Pasteur was a **microbiologist.** He became famous for his studies of microbes. He made many discoveries that have led to cures for diseases in both humans and animals. He also discovered ways to preserve foods for longer periods of time.

A. Early Life
Louis Pasteur was born on December 27, 1822, in Dole, France. His father, an ex-soldier, loved to read history to his son. Louis probably got his great love for learning from him. However, Louis was not an exceptional student in school and preferred to spend time on his own interests.

As a teenager, Louis had a talent for painting. His family assumed he would be an artist. However, Louis ended up studying science at the world famous Ecole Normale Superieure in Paris. He earned his doctoral degree in 1847.

While at school, Pasteur became especially interested in studying crystals. He continued his experiments after others might have given up. His talents let him see connections and make discoveries that others did not see.

B. Pasteurization

By 1854, Pasteur had become a professor at the University of Strasbourg at Lille, France. An alcohol manufacturer asked for his help with a **fermentation** problem. Sometimes during the process, the wine soured.

Yeast is the microbe that turns sugar into alcohol. Pasteur discovered that the good wine was full of round yeast cells. The sour wine was full of oval-shaped ones. These oblong cells were forcing the round ones out and turning the wine sour. These cells proved that some microbes were helpful and some were harmful.

In his laboratory, Louis Pasteur discovered a cure for rabies and developed the process of pasteurization to protect food.

Pasteur also proved that fermentation was a living process. He discovered that heating the wine to a certain temperature would kill the harmful yeast cells and prevent souring. Pasteur tried his heating **theory** on other liquids, including milk. Heating it kept the milk from souring so quickly. This heating process, called **pasteurization,** is still used today to protect milk and other foods.

C. Germ Therapy

In the mid-1800s, many people believed in **spontaneous generation.** For example, people believed that a maggot or a worm could grow out of a dead animal's body. Many scientists believed in spontaneous generation too. Pasteur proved that spontaneous generation was a false idea. He did this by finding the real source for the unexpected appearance of small animals.

Pasteur became more famous with each successful experiment. By the early 1860s, Pasteur was known as the leading chemist in the world.

In 1865, the French government asked him to help the French silk industry. The silkworms were having trouble making good silk. After working for three years, Pasteur discovered that a microbe was infecting the silkworms. When the infected worms were destroyed, the problem disappeared.

The silkworm project led to the **germ** theory of disease, one of the most important medical discoveries of all time. This discovery was the first insight to the cause of many diseases. Scientists now knew that germs were harmful microscopic organisms that caused disease.

Although he was famous and honored, Pasteur experienced serious health problems. At the age of 46, Pasteur suffered a stroke that caused paralysis in his left arm and leg. Still, he continued his work.

D. Cures for Rabies and Chicken Cholera
Pasteur discovered that harmful microbes caused chicken cholera. In 1880, Pasteur grew some of these germs. He noticed that they became weaker as time passed. He tried injecting the weakened microbes into the chickens. He found that this injection raised the ability of the chickens to fight the disease.

Pasteur's most dramatic success came when he turned his vaccination techniques to **rabies.** This **fatal** disease was spread by animal bites. He noticed that nerve tissues from **rabid** animals weakened as they dried. He injected the weakened tissues into a dog. Each day he injected the dog with stronger tissues. After 14 days, the dog showed no sign of rabies. On July 6, 1885, he tried his vaccination on a dying boy who had been bitten by a rabid dog. The boy lived.

Summary
Following the success of the rabies vaccine, international funds were raised to open the Pasteur Institute for the further study of rabies. Pasteur headed the institute from its dedication in 1888 until his death on September 28, 1895. Writings on the walls of the institute tell of Pasteur's many accomplishments.

Read and Record: Place the following dates on the timeline:
(1) Louis Pasteur's birth
(2) Silkworm problem solved
(3) Pasteur uses first rabies vaccine
(4) Louis Pasteur's death
(5) Edward Jenner's death
(6) Vacuum cleaner invented (1901)
(7) Your birth date
(8) First smallpox vaccination

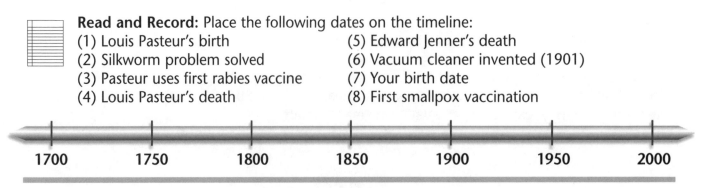

1700   1750   1800   1850   1900   1950   2000

Review: Fill in this Main Idea chart. Write a title that captures the overall meaning of the article. List the four sections and write three main ideas about each section.

	Title			
A.				
B.				
C.				
D.				

 Rethink: Answer each of the following questions.

1. Why did the French government think Pasteur could help solve the silkworm problem?

_____

_____

2. How were the chicken cholera and rabies cures related?

_____

_____

React and Write: Answer this question with a drawing.

1. Draw three microscopic wine samples. Make one that is good, one that is souring, and one that is sour.

Paul Ehrlich   (1854–1915)

Preview: Look through the text. Find the author's subject and main topics. Do this by looking at the title of the article and the boldface headings marked A, B, C, and D. Use this information to predict the main idea of this article.

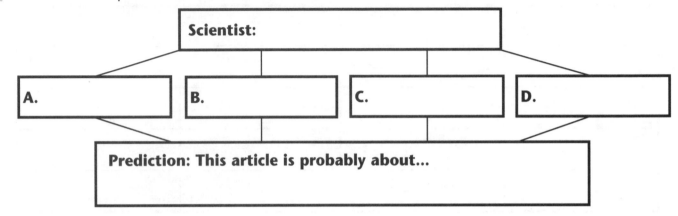

Scientist:

A.

B.

C.

D.

Prediction: This article is probably about...

Prepare: Match each definition with the correct word. Use the glossary if you need help.

_____	1. use of chemicals to prevent or treat disease	**a.** tuberculosis
_____	2. strange and unusual person	**b.** bacteria
_____	3. disease that affects the lungs	**c.** syphilis
_____	4. to control so that all are alike	**d.** standardize
_____	5. microscopic matter that causes disease	**e.** eccentric
_____	6. disease that was deadly before 1900	**f.** chemotherapy

Paul Ehrlich

Paul Ehrlich was a medical researcher. He spent his life studying the way human bodies fight disease. Ehrlich invented the word **chemotherapy.** He was especially interested in studying blood. In 1908, he received the Nobel Prize because his experiments added greatly to scientific knowledge.

A. Early Life
Ehrlich was born on March 14, 1854, in Strehlen, Germany. At school, Paul's record was inconsistent. He was excellent in mathematics and Latin but almost failed composition. When he got to Breslau University, he made two important decisions: to become a doctor and to study dyes.

He was interested in using dyes to stain living tissues so they would be easier to identify and study. However, he was more interested in his dye experiments than in school. It took him four universities and an extra year to earn his medical degree from the University of Leipzig in 1878.

B. Tissue Dyes and Tuberculosis

Ehrlich spent the next six years as a doctor in Berlin. Many odd personal habits earned him a reputation as an **eccentric.** But he was too involved in his tissue studies to notice. He learned that some dyes stain tissues and some do not. He found that some dyes stain only one type of tissue. Eventually, he discovered a method of staining cells that helped him to find and identify the five different types of white blood cells.

This staining method helped to make the microscopic matter that causes **tuberculosis (TB)** visible. Ehrlich's basic methods are still used today. Tuberculosis at that time was a feared disease that took many lives. As a matter of fact, Ehrlich himself got a mild case of TB, probably from his work. He went to Egypt for two years, where he recovered.

Paul Ehrlich's staining methods helped to make tuberculosis bacteria visible. He also worked on cures for other diseases.

C. Diphtheria and Side-Chain Theory

Next, Ehrlich turned his attention to **diphtheria,** a deadly children's disease. He began to work with Robert Koch, a scientist who had isolated the TB **bacteria.** He also worked with Emil von Behring in diphtheria research.

The main problem with curing diphtheria was that treatments varied in strength. Ehrlich developed a way to **standardize** these treatments so they would be neither too strong nor too weak.

While experimenting on the diphtheria cure, Ehrlich discovered that cells have **side-chains.** These are cell attachments that do not control the work of the cell, but are needed for the cell to live. This discovery opened the door to experiments with specific cell and treatment combinations.

D. Magic Bullet and Syphilis

In 1896, Ehrlich became director of the State Institute for Serum Research and Control at Steiglitz in Berlin, Germany. Here he was free to experiment on his own. He worked hard. Sometimes he even forgot to eat. He took a few days off. Still considered an eccentric, he worked in incredibly cluttered laboratories. He talked excitedly and wrote on anything available. It was a happy and productive time for him.

Ehrlich wanted to find what he called a *magic bullet.* This substance would kill bacteria but not harm the body. His search for this magic bullet led to hundreds of failures. No real progress occurred for years. Finally, he and Dr. Sahachiro Hata found success while searching for a cure for sleeping sickness. The 606th experiment was rejected. Later, they looked at it again and found it was a cure for **syphilis.** The 914th sleeping sickness experiment proved to be a second cure for syphilis.

The 606th experiment, conducted in 1907, became the magic bullet. It was called 606 or Salvarsan (that which saves by arsenic). Its effect on dying syphilis patients was very fast. This new cure was announced to the world in 1910.

Summary

Ehrlich's side-chain theory led to the cures of both diphtheria and syphilis. These successes were the first proof that chemicals could be used to fight microbes. The search could now begin for drugs to fight other diseases. When Ehrlich died five years later, on August 20, 1915, he was still researching new drugs.

Paul Ehrlich's life is an example of how hard work and persistence can lead to success. His work is important because his experiments resulted in saving many lives and paved the way for saving millions of people from diseases. His method of developing cures opened up new fields of research and prepared the way for other medical successes in the twentieth century.

Read and Record: Place the following dates on the timeline:

(1) Paul Ehrlich's birth
(2) Side-chain theory work begins
(3) Syphilis cure announced
(4) Paul Ehrlich's death

(5) First rabies vaccine
(6) Louis Pasteur's death
(7) Your birth date
(8) Jimmy Carter becomes President (1977)

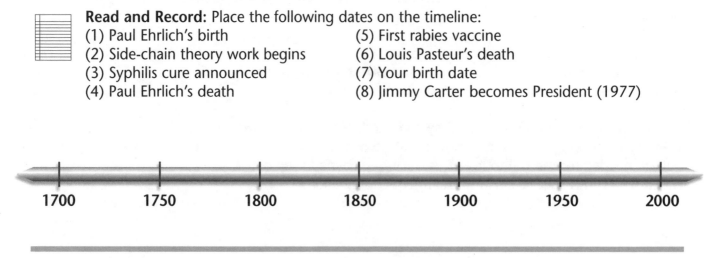

1700   1750   1800   1850   1900   1950   2000

Review: Fill in this Main Idea chart. Write a title that captures the overall meaning of the article. List the four sections of the article and write three main ideas about each section.

	Title			
A.				
B.				
C.				
D.				

Rethink: Answer each of the following questions.

1. Describe two research discoveries that Ehrlich made.

_____

_____

2. What did Ehrlich mean by the term *magic bullet*?

_____

_____

React and Write: Answer this question with a complete sentence.

1. How have modern-day people benefited from Ehrlich's eccentric nature?

_____

_____

_____

_____

_____

UNIT 1

Alexander Fleming (1881–1955)

Preview: Look through the text. Find the author's subject and main topics. Do this by looking at the title of the article and the boldface headings marked A, B, C, and D. Use this information to predict the main idea of this article.

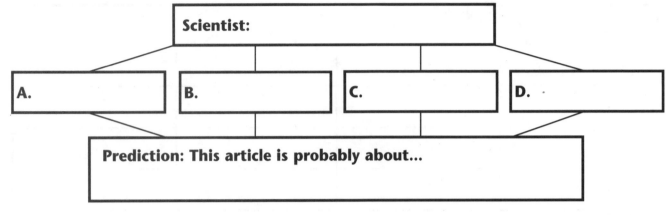

Scientist:

A.

B.

C.

D.

Prediction: This article is probably about...

Prepare: Match each definition with the correct word. Use the glossary if you need help.

_____ 1. scientist who studies bacteria	**a.** petri dish
_____ 2. drug made from mold used to treat disease	**b.** penicillin
_____ 3. substance made in living organisms that causes change	**c.** bacteriologist
_____ 4. able destroy bacteria	**d.** antibiotic
_____ 5. a shallow dish with a loose-fitting cover; used in labs	**e.** enzyme
_____ 6. a living substance used to prevent or treat disease	**f.** antibacterial

Alexander Fleming

Alexander Fleming was an English **bacteriologist** who discovered **penicillin.** This discovery was an accident. In fact, many events in Fleming's life were simply products of chance. When he received an honor from Harvard University, Fleming said, "It is perfectly wonderful what a part chance or fate or fortune or destiny—whatever you like to call it—plays in our lives."

A. Early Life
Alexander Fleming was born in southern Scotland on August 6, 1881. He was a bright, curious child who loved to explore. When he was 13, he went to London to live with his older brother Tom, a beginning doctor. By the age of 15, Alexander was working as a clerk in a shipping office.

A series of chance events then changed the course of Alexander's life. Unexpectedly, he inherited some money from an uncle and decided to go back to school. He was an excellent student. When he decided to enter medical school, he could pick the school of his choice. He had played water polo at St. Mary's College, so he picked that school. He chose to be a surgeon because of a remark made by a friend. When it was time for him to begin practice, a member of the St. Mary's rifle team got him a job in St. Mary's lab because the rifle team needed a sharpshooter. Even though he was trained as a surgeon, he spent the rest of his life studying bacteria in a lab. It was in a laboratory that he would make his most famous discovery.

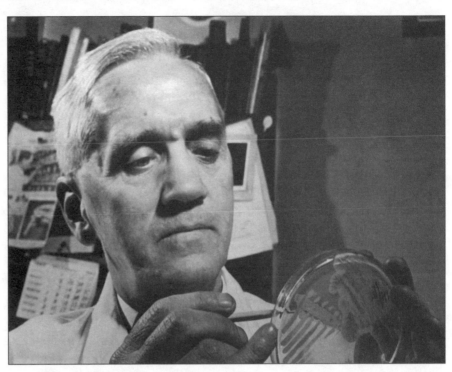

Alexander Fleming saw that something in the mucus killed bacteria. His chance finding led to the discovery of penicillin.

B. Private 606 and WWI

In 1909, Paul Ehrlich, a German scientist, discovered a cure for syphilis. (see Lesson 3) The cure was known as Salvarsan, or 606. Fleming became one of the few London doctors to treat syphilis patients with Salvarsan. Fleming developed such a busy practice with syphilis patients that he was nicknamed "Private 606."

During World War I, Fleming worked in a French military hospital. He felt helpless when soldiers died from simple infections. In his army lab, he worked on ways to fight bacteria. He found no way to help these soldiers.

After the war was over, Fleming continued to look for a cure for the types of infections the soldiers had. One day in 1921, Fleming had a cold. He put some of his own mucus in a **petri dish.** This led Fleming to discover the **enzyme** called lysozyme. Fleming noticed this enzyme had a natural **antibacterial** effect. It had killed the cold bacteria. Fleming continued to research for the next seven years, looking for a chemical that could fight microbes in wounds.

C. Penicillin Discovery

In 1928, Fleming put some deadly staph germs in a petri dish. He forgot about the dish until two weeks later. Then, he saw that some green mold had grown on the dish. He also noticed that there was no bacteria in the area of the mold. Fleming called this mold penicillin. It was able to kill the staph germs without harming healthy cells. Other known treatments were sometimes more dangerous to healthy cells than to bacteria cells.

D. Finishing the Task

Supplying the drug was difficult. All forms of the drug were still grown from the original mold in Fleming's petri dish. Forty gallons of mold were needed to make enough penicillin for one patient for one day. Fleming turned the production problem over to a group of chemists. Some of the chemists died and others relocated. This caused the work to stop.

When World War II started, interest in curing infections grew. Two Oxford chemists, Dr. Ernst Chain and Dr. Howard Florey, continued Fleming's work. They learned that penicillin acts by not letting bacteria build cell walls. This stops the spread of bacteria. Since animal cells do not have cell walls, they are not hurt by penicillin. This greater understanding of the process was helpful. Penicillin was finally ready for use in the 1940s, more than ten years after Fleming's discovery. A United States Department of Agriculture laboratory worked on the supply problem. By 1945, more than a thousand pounds of penicillin were produced every month. Penicillin became the first successful **antibiotic** and was widely used to cure soldiers in WWII. Since then, penicillin has saved millions of people from death by infection.

Summary

Along with Doctors Chain and Florey, Fleming received the Nobel Prize for medicine. Fleming was also given an honorary degree from Harvard University. When he died in 1955, he had begun the chain of discoveries of antibiotics that made it possible for doctors to cure many diseases. How lucky for the world that so many chance events led Alexander Fleming on the road to bacteriology!

Read and Record: Place the following dates on the timeline:

(1) Alexander Fleming's birth   (5) Syphilis cure announced
(2) Penicillin is ready for use   (6) Boeing 707 introduced (1958)
(3) Penicillin is first discovered   (7) Your birth date
(4) Alexander Fleming's death   (8) Bayer aspirin introduced (1900)

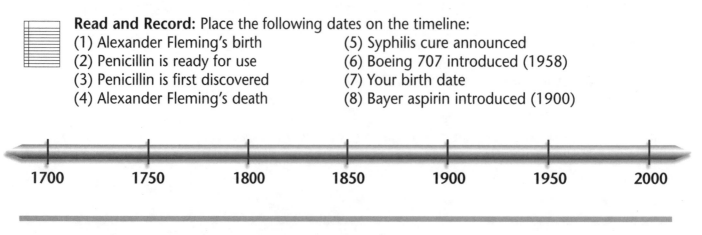

| 1700 | 1750 | 1800 | 1850 | 1900 | 1950 | 2000 |

Review: Fill in this Main Idea chart. Write a title that captures the overall meaning of the article. List the four sections and write three main ideas about each section.

	Title			
A.				
B.				
C.				
D.				

 Rethink: Answer each of the following questions.

1. What part did World Wars I and II play in the discovery of penicillin?

_____

_____

2. Explain why Fleming's discovery of penicillin was largely due to fate.

_____

_____

React and Write: Answer this question with a drawing.

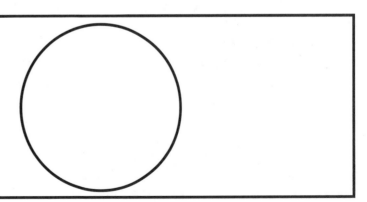

1. Draw a picture of the mucus and mold that Fleming found in the petri dish. Use your imagination and details from the story.

Frederick Grant Banting   (1891-1941)

Preview: Look through the text. Find the author's subject and main topics. Do this by looking at the title of the article and the boldface headings marked A, B, C, and D. Use this information to predict the main idea of this article.

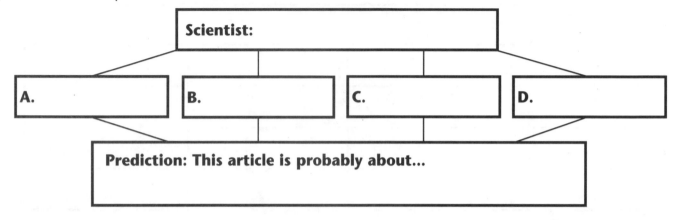

Scientist:

A.

B.

C.

D.

Prediction: This article is probably about...

Prepare: Match each definition with the correct word. Use the glossary if you need help.

_____ 1. disease in which the body cannot use sugar   **a.** insulin

_____ 2. substance that controls blood sugar levels in the body   **b.** lecturer

_____ 3. reaction or condition caused by disease   **c.** affliction

_____ 4. to surgically remove   **d.** diabetes

_____ 5. one who gives speeches to teach people   **e.** symptom

_____ 6. disease   **f.** amputate

Frederick Grant Banting

Frederick Grant Banting was a Canadian biologist who helped thousands of **diabetes** sufferers live near-normal lives. The victims of diabetes are unable to use food sugars. Sufferers used to starve to death, no matter what they ate. Banting discovered **insulin** and changed the lives of diabetics. In 1923, Banting received a Nobel Prize for his discovery.

A. Early Life
Frederick Grant Banting was born on November 14, 1891, in Alliston, Ontario, Canada. One of his childhood friends died of diabetes at the age of 14. Banting was so upset that he decided to become a doctor. He wanted to try to cure the horrible **affliction** that took his friend from him.

In 1912, he entered the University of Toronto Medical School. He received excellent grades, but he had to work very hard for them.

During World War I, Banting did hospital work in England and France. He was shot in the arm and surgeons insisted that the arm be **amputated.** However, Banting refused to let them take off his arm. Luckily, it healed.

B. Pancreas Connection

After the war, Banting set up an office as a surgeon in London, Ontario. He also worked a part-time job as a **lecturer** at the University of Western Ontario. One night he was preparing notes for a lecture on the **pancreas.** He knew that this small organ is located behind the stomach and makes digestive juices that help break up food to be absorbed into the bloodstream. He also knew that when the pancreas is removed from dogs, the animals get diabetes and die within weeks.

As he prepared this lecture, Banting wondered about the health of pancreases in humans with diabetes. He found some research results on a single victim. The body's pancreas was normal except for one small cluster of cells.

Frederick Grant Banting sold his personal belongings to finance early research for insulin to help people with diabetes.

He knew past researchers had tried to help diabetes victims fight the disease by giving them some healthy pancreas cells. However, they had no success. Banting decided to experiment.

C. Surgeon Turned Researcher

Banting was a surgeon. He had no research money and no laboratory. In 1920, he went to see Professor J. J. R. Macleod at the University of Toronto Medical School. This man was famous for his research on sugar in the body. Macleod was not impressed, but Banting persisted. Banting asked for a trial period: eight weeks in a lab, ten dogs, and an assistant. Macleod reluctantly agreed.

By May of 1921, Banting was working with Charles W. Best, an unpaid student assistant. Their plan was to tie the pancreas tubes in the dogs. They hoped to see what effect this would have on insulin. A lack of money made it necessary for Banting to sell his car and other personal belongings. He did not give up— even though it was summer and the laboratory was in a hot, stuffy upstairs room.

Then in late July, insulin helped a dog to recover after nearly dying from diabetes. Unfortunately, the dog died the following day. The two men were disappointed and confused. They eventually learned that insulin can only relieve the **symptoms** of diabetes. It is not a cure. To live, victims must continue to take the substance daily.

D. Success and Fame
Problems persisted. Banting did not want to kill healthy dogs to get insulin. He switched to unborn cows thrown away at slaughterhouses. By now, it was past the eight-week trial period. Luckily, Macleod was out of the country. The two scientists continued working. When Macleod returned, he was impressed enough with their work to allow them to stay in his lab.

Dr. Joe Gilchrist, one of Banting's former medical school classmates, suffered from diabetes. He was willing to let Banting experiment on him. Soon, many desperate diabetics traveled to Canada for help. Eventually, Banting gave the rights to produce insulin to the university because he wanted a safe supply.

When the 1923 Nobel Prize was awarded to Macleod and Banting, Banting was outraged. He publicly credited Best, and shared the prize money with him. Nine months later, Macleod gave a statement to a Toronto newspaper crediting Banting and Best with the work.

Summary
With persistence and humility, Banting continued to work hard. His sudden death in a plane crash occurred on Feb. 21, 1941, while he was serving in World War II. But thanks to him, insulin has saved many lives.

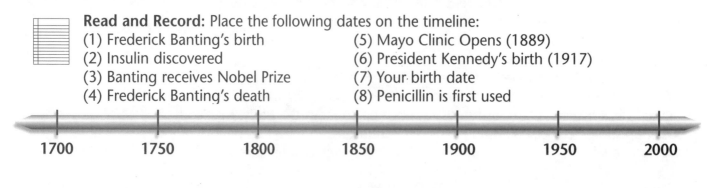

Read and Record: Place the following dates on the timeline:
(1) Frederick Banting's birth	(5) Mayo Clinic Opens (1889)
(2) Insulin discovered	(6) President Kennedy's birth (1917)
(3) Banting receives Nobel Prize	(7) Your birth date
(4) Frederick Banting's death	(8) Penicillin is first used

1700   1750   1800   1850   1900   1950   2000

Review: Fill in this Main Idea chart. Write a title that captures the overall meaning of the article. List the four sections and write three main ideas about each section.

	Title			
A.				
B.				
C.				
D.				

Rethink: Answer each of the following questions.

1. Why did Banting and Best's first insulin-treated dog die?

_____

_____

2. What does the pancreas have to do with diabetes?

_____

_____

React and Write: Plan diabetic meals for one day.

Diabetics eat controlled diets. One idea of a diabetic diet is to eat very little from group #1, one daily serving from group #2, and three servings from each of groups #3 and #4. Using this plan, make a one-day diabetic menu.

Group #1—Potatoes and breads   Group #3—Green vegetables
Group #2—Fruits and non-green vegetables   Group #4—Meats and Cheeses

Breakfast	Lunch	Dinner

Experiment: Using Iodine to Search for Starch

Challenge
As you have learned, Paul Ehrlich found that varied tissues react differently to like solutions. For example, when items containing starch are treated with iodine, they will turn black. Do the following experiment to understand a little about how Dr. Ehrlich collected data.

Materials (per experiment)
1" piece of celery	1/4 slice of bread	1 plant leaf or a handful of grass
1" cube of raw potato	1 small cracker	3 inch square of paper
paper towels	iodine with dropper	

Procedure
Place the celery, bread, leaf or grass, potato, cracker, and paper each on a separate paper towel. Place three drops of iodine on each of the six items.

Hypothesis
Record your expectations in the chart below.

celery	bread
leaf or grass	potato
cracker	paper

Results
Record your results in the chart below.

celery	bread
leaf or grass	potato
cracker	paper

Conclusion
Based on your procedure and results, which items contained starch? How can you tell?

_____

_____

_____

_____

Making Connections: Details and Sequencing

In Unit 2, Making Connections, you will learn about five life scientists who tried to see the larger picture. They worked to connect their science with larger issues. They realized that all knowledge is connected.

In this unit, you will read about the scientist who first set up a logical system of naming plants so that many scientists all over the world could share knowledge. Then, you will learn about the researcher who organized animals into categories. Next, you will meet the biologist whose controversial ideas are still discussed and argued about today. Fourth, you will read about the man who discovered the basic laws of **heredity.** Finally, you will learn about the science writer who raised the conscience of a nation with her books. These five scientists all had to work hard to overcome personal difficulties in order to succeed in their discoveries of the basic connections in life.

While you are reading about these scientists, you will also be considering the importance of details and sequencing. In Unit 1, you considered the main idea of each **biography.** Without details to prove and develop that main idea, it would be incomplete. Without a logical arrangement and sequence of those details, you would not be able to follow the author's arguments. Both details and sequence are important.

You can expect to learn about a main idea in the introduction, headings, and opening sentences of a selection. Several details will follow such main idea statements. In addition, the main idea statement will give you hints about what kind of details you can expect. For example, if the main idea statement tells you there are many reasons for an event, you can expect a list of reasons to follow. This unit will give you practice in making connections as you read.

 When you are finished with this unit, place one significant date for each scientist you have learned about on this timeline.

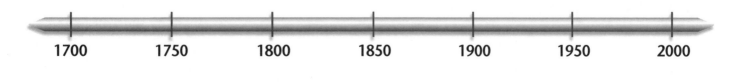

1700   1750   1800   1850   1900   1950   2000

Carolus Linnaeus   (1707–1778)

Preview: Look through the text. Find the author's subject and main topics. Do this by looking at the title of the article and the boldface headings marked A, B, C, and D. Use this information to predict the main idea of this article.

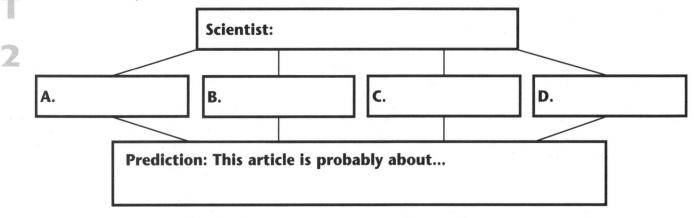

Scientist:

A.

B.

C.

D.

Prediction: This article is probably about...

Prepare: Match each definition with the correct word. Use the glossary if you need help.

_____ **1.** scientist who studies plants

_____ **2.** grouping into categories by shared features

_____ **3.** sample; small part of a larger group

_____ **4.** system of naming organisms

_____ **5.** group of similar life forms that cannot mate with each other

_____ **6.** group of similar life forms that can mate with each other

a. binomial nomenclature

b. specimen

c. species

d. genus

e. botanist

f. classification

Carolus Linnaeus

Carolus Linnaeus was a Swedish **botanist.** He established a system of classification of plants, animals, and minerals. He had a strong influence on **botany** by assigning a Latin name to each plant. Because of his use of Latin, he became famous as Carolus Linnaeus rather than as Carl von Linné, his birth name.

A. Early Life
Carl von Linné was born on May 23, 1707, in South Rashult, Sweden. Because he was interested in plants from early childhood, he was called "the little botanist" at the age of eight.

Although Carl seemed interested only in plants, he ended up studying medicine. He wanted to teach and, at that time, nobody could teach in Sweden without a medical degree. During his schooling, he remained more interested in botany than in medicine.

By 1730, he was a poor student lecturing on botany. He began to write his observations in journals. In 1732, he received a $50 gift from the Royal Society. With this money, he was able to spend five months collecting plants in Lapland.

B. Language Problem

As Linnaeus wrote about plants, he became frustrated because botanists had no common language. Scientists all over the world were studying plants. However, they were using different names for the same plants. It was difficult to share knowledge.

In 1735, Linnaeus published *Systema Naturae* (System of Nature). In this book, he introduced a new system of **classification** so that all scientists would use the same words. He based his system on the makeup of flowers. Within a flower's petals is a **stamen**, a long stem covered with a yellow powder called **pollen.** Each grain of pollen is a male reproductive cell. In the center of the flower is a **pistil** with the flower's female reproductive cell at its bottom. When the pollen meets the pistil, seeds result.

Carolus Linnaeus developed binomial nomenclature. This classification system gave scientists a common language.

Linnaeus changed the way botanists looked at plants. Previously, scientists thought that the roots, stems, and branches were what mattered. Linnaeus based his classification on the number of stamens and pistils in a flower. The system was simple but very logical.

C. Binomial Nomenclature

By the time *Systema Naturae* was published, Linnaeus had received his medical degree in Holland. He studied and wrote there for three years. In 1738, he returned to Sweden to practice medicine. Three years later, he became a professor at the University of Uppsala. He remained there for the rest of his life. He continued to classify new **specimens** and to correspond with botanists from all over the world.

In 1753, Linnaeus published *Species Plantarum.* In this work, he set up his most important contribution, **binomial nomenclature.** Binomial comes from the Latin words for two (bi), and name (nomen). He identified every plant by two names. The first name is its **genus,** the group to which it belongs. The second is its **species,** a specific description. Six years later, he introduced the same system for the animal world. For example, in this system all cats have the same genus, *felis.* A lion is *Felis leo,* a tiger is *Felis tigris,* and a leopard is *Felis pardus.* The second word in the name is the species, which tells the kind of cat.

D. Later Years

Scholars soon recognized the importance of a such a universal system. Linnaeus became a famous man. Assisted by his son Carl, Linnaeus continued his work. Within Linnaeus' more than 180 publications was included the classification of humans as *Homo sapiens,* which means "man, wise." He was also the first to use the ♂ symbol for man and the ♀ symbol for woman. Linnaeus' system was being used throughout the world of science when he died on January 10, 1778.

Summary

Linnaeus gave scientists an ordered, official, and international system of classification. This system provided the tools to make connections and to advance science worldwide. Without his system, other scientists interested in generalizations would have been unable to do their great work. Linnaeus' descriptive method, standard names, and practical method are still in use today. His work supplied the necessary foundation for modern science.

Read and Record: Place the following dates on the timeline:

(1) Carolus Linnaeus' birth
(2) First nomenclature book published
(3) *Species Plantarum* published
(4) Carolus Linnaeus' death
(5) Frederick Banting's death
(6) President Lincoln's birth (1809)
(7) Your birth date
(8) Boston Tea Party (1773)

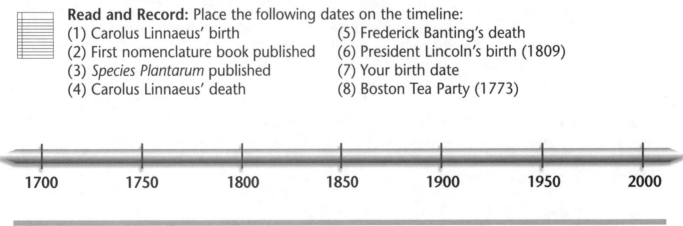

1700 1750 1800 1850 1900 1950 2000

Review: Fill in this sequence/detail chart. Cover four main stages of the scientist's life. Identify three related details for each.

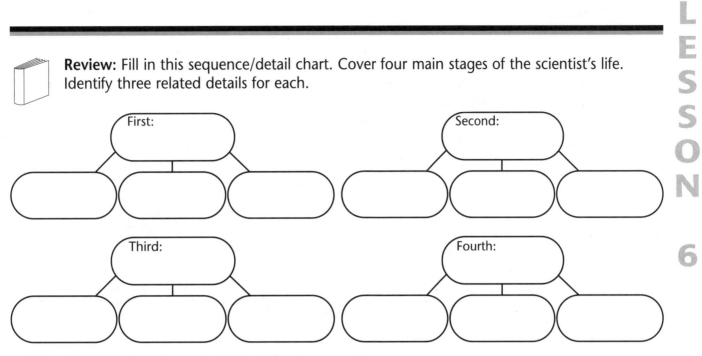

First:

Second:

Third:

Fourth:

Rethink: Answer each of the following questions.

1. Why was binomial nomenclature an important contribution to the world of science?

_____

_____

2. What is the difference between Linnaeus' *Systema Naturae* and his *Species Plantarum*?

_____

_____

React and Write: Use a reference book to find the binomial nomenclature for each animal.

1. dog _____

2. zebra _____

3. horse_____

4. snapping turtle _____

5. bald eagle _____

Jean Baptiste Lamarck   (1744–1829)

Preview: Look through the text. Find the author's subject and main topics. Do this by looking at the title of the article and the boldface headings marked A, B, C, and D. Use this information to predict the main idea of this article.

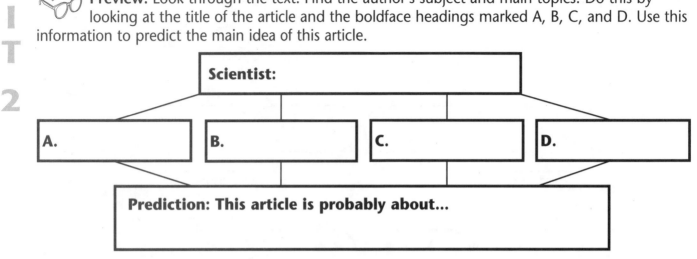

Prepare: Match each definition with the correct word. Use the glossary if you need help.

_____ 1. animal that has a backbone	**a.** evolution
_____ 2. animal that does not have a backbone	**b.** aristocrat
_____ 3. gradual change of a group of organisms	**c.** civilian
_____ 4. member of the ruling family	**d.** ridicule
_____ 5. person who is not in the military	**e.** vertebrate
_____ 6. to make fun of	**f.** invertebrate

Jean Baptiste Lamarck

Jean Baptiste Lamarck did not start his real life's work until he was over 30 years old. When he did become a botanist, he made the distinction between **vertebrates** and **invertebrates**. Lamarck also set up ideas that would start scientists thinking about **evolution**.

A. Early Life
Jean Baptiste Lamarck was born on August 1, 1744, in the city of Bazantin, Picardy, France. He was the youngest son of 11 children. His family was a very old and noble one, but it was also poor. In families of **aristocrats** at that time, only two possibilities existed for sons who could not inherit family money: they could enter the church or the army.

At first, against his will, Lamarck was destined for the church. When his father died in 1760, Jean Baptiste changed directions and joined the army. He was a good soldier and fought in the Seven Years War. He was even honored for bravery, but ill health forced him back into **civilian** life in 1768.

B. Career Steps

Lamarck spent the next few years in Paris. He worked at a variety of jobs from bank clerking to tutoring. He still had very little money. Botany began to interest him and he spent a great deal of time studying on his own.

Lamarck's life changed in 1778. He published a book on French flowers and was admitted into the French Academy of Sciences. Other scientists now saw him as an authority on botany. Three years after the publication of his book, Lamarck was named as botanist to King Louis XVI. Now he had a salary.

Finally, in 1793, he was hired as a professor at the Museum of Natural History in Paris. Although he had no knowledge in the area, Lamarck was put

Lamarck's work formed the basis of invertebrate study. He also paved the way for Charles Darwin's theory of evolution.

in charge of insects and worms. At that time, little was known about insects. Lamarck decided to take on the job of classifying these small animals. In doing this classification, he made his greatest contribution to science.

C. Vertebrates and Invertebrates

Lamarck began to investigate the tiny animals at the museum. He classified the animals by noting whether they had a bony spine. If they did, he called them vertebrates. If they did not, they were invertebrates. In his classification, he identified many types of invertebrates. For example, he classified eight-legged spiders as arachnids. Between 1815 and 1822, he produced the seven-volume *Natural History of Invertebrate Animals.* This book set the foundation for modern invertebrate **zoology.**

Zoology is the study of animals, and botany is the study of plants. Lamarck saw the need to study all living things as a whole. He created the word **biology** to include the study of all living things, plant and animal.

D. Theory of Evolution

In 1809, Lamarck published an important essay called *Zoological Philosophy*. In this work, he became the first respected biologist to suggest the idea that life on Earth is constantly changing and developing. Lamarck believed that plants and animals change their forms to adapt to their surroundings. He also believed that they pass on these changes to their offspring. This idea was a theory, an idea which needed to be proved.

Unfortunately, Lamarck's proof was not very convincing. His examples were poor and not based on factual evidence. His most famous examples involved giraffes and ducks. He theorized that antelopes stretching their necks to get food would end up as giraffes hundreds of years later. He also theorized that birds spreading their feet when they landed on water would eventually become ducks.

Lamarck's theory of evolution was either ignored or **ridiculed** by other scientists. Despite this, Lamarck continued his work. Although scientists were laughing, they were still being forced to think about the idea that life on Earth does indeed change—even if it changed differently from how Lamarck described it.

Summary

Jean Baptiste Lamarck had a difficult life. Much of it was lived in poverty. Late in life, he became blind. Still, he never gave up his work. He continued by dictating to one of his daughters. By the time he died on December 28, 1829, he was not only blind but also poor. However, Lamarck's work formed the basis of invertebrate study. Also, he paved the way for Charles Darwin's theory of evolution 30 years later. For a mostly self-taught scientist, Lamarck's accomplishments were many.

Read and Record: Place the following dates on the timeline:
(1) Jean Baptiste Lamarck's birth
(2) Lamarck begins classifying insects
(3) *Zoological Philosophy* published
(4) Jean Baptiste Lamarck's death
(5) First smallpox vaccination
(6) President Reagan's birth (1911)
(7) Your birth date
(8) First nomenclature book published

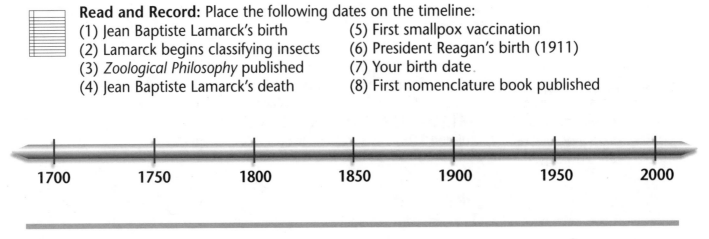

1700   1750   1800   1850   1900   1950   2000

Review: Fill in this sequence/detail chart. Cover four main stages of the scientist's life. Identify three related details for each.

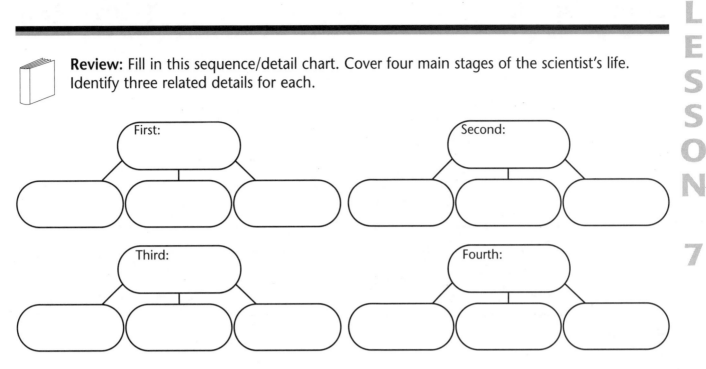

First:

Second:

Third:

Fourth:

Rethink: Answer each of the following questions.

1. Lamarck is remembered as an important scientist. Why would people continue to respect a person who believed antelopes could turn into giraffes?

_____

_____

2. What was the point in identifying animals as either vertebrates or invertebrates?

_____

_____

React and Write: Lay out the sequence of events in Lamarck's life. Record one event for each age on the line.

age → | 16   24   34 37   49   65   71   78   85

Charles Darwin   (1809–1882)

Preview: Look through the text. Find the author's subject and main topics. Do this by looking at the title of the article and the boldface headings marked A, B, C, and D. Use this information to predict the main idea of this article.

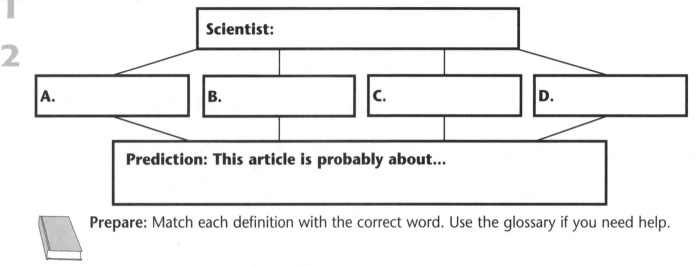

Scientist:

A.

B.

C.

D.

Prediction: This article is probably about...

Prepare: Match each definition with the correct word. Use the glossary if you need help.

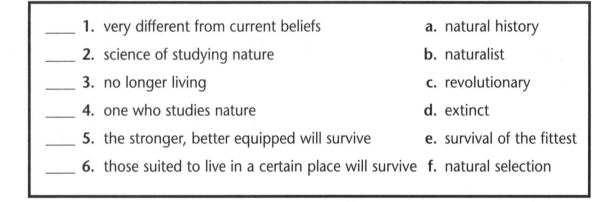

____ 1. very different from current beliefs	**a.** natural history
____ 2. science of studying nature	**b.** naturalist
____ 3. no longer living	**c.** revolutionary
____ 4. one who studies nature	**d.** extinct
____ 5. the stronger, better equipped will survive	**e.** survival of the fittest
____ 6. those suited to live in a certain place will survive	**f.** natural selection

Charles Darwin

Charles Darwin is famous for his **revolutionary** theory of evolution. This idea caused controversy when he proposed it, and it causes controversy today. However, Darwin was a gentle, hard-working man who loved **natural history.** He tried to make important connections and answer basic questions.

A. Early Life
Charles Darwin was born on February 12, 1809, in Shrewsbury, England. He was welcomed into a very famous family. His father Robert was a respected doctor. One grandfather was a famous poet and physician. The other was the well-to-do Josiah Wedgwood, who was famous for his pottery.

When Darwin was young, he was only interested in natural history. He received poor grades in school. He did not want to learn Greek or Latin. He was sent to the University of Edinburgh to study medicine. However, he hated it, especially when he saw surgery without relief from pain.

Then Darwin learned that he had an inheritance. He no longer needed to work. He left the university and enrolled in Christ's College to study for the ministry. He earned a degree in 1831 even though he was not happy there.

B. A Trip on the Beagle

In 1831, Darwin took a job on a ship called *H.M.S. Beagle* that was about to travel to South America and sail around the world. Darwin would make scientific observations and collect specimens. The voyage took five years, and it got Darwin started on the career that would make him famous.

Darwin collected and labeled specimens, took notes, and wrote in journals. Whenever the ship landed, he sent a shipment to England. The crates carried his collected plants, fossils, insects, flowers, birds, and animals.

In Argentina, he found fossil remains of **extinct** animals. In Chile, he saw active volcanoes. The idea of a changing Earth began to interest him more and more. Then, Darwin went to the Galapagos Islands off the coast of Ecuador in South America. There he found giant tortoises that existed no place else on Earth. He also found 14 varieties of a finch. Those varieties did not exist anywhere else. He believed those birds must have **evolved** on the islands. He would spend the next 25 years of his life studying these findings.

Charles Darwin's theories on survival of the fittest and natural selection created a controversy: Did humans evolve, too?

C. The Theory of Evolution

When Darwin returned to England in 1836, he learned that some of his papers had been published while he was on board the *Beagle.* He was already regarded as a leading **naturalist.**

Jean Baptiste Lamarck (see Lesson 7) was ridiculed for presenting theories of evolution. Darwin made the idea of evolution more acceptable. He based his theories on scientific explanations rather than unfounded fancy. Lamarck said that antelopes became giraffes because they tried to stretch their necks. Darwin, on the other hand, theorized that some giraffes were actually born with longer necks. These giraffes were more successful in the struggle for existence. They got the most food, lived longer, and produced stronger offspring. Passing on the valuable difference of a longer neck, their children would be the ones to survive. Eventually, those with shorter necks would die out. Since only those that were more fit would survive, Darwin thought that evolution was accomplished through **survival of the fittest**.

Another part of Darwin's theory is **natural selection.** Darwin believed that some varieties of a species—like a giraffe with a longer neck or a finch with a spoon-shaped beak—would be more suited to life in a specific place. Those more suited would survive. The others would die out. It was almost as if nature had selected some variations to survive in certain environments.

D. The Controversy Begins

After years of classifying, questioning, and writing, Darwin published *The Origin of Species* in 1859. Six editions quickly sold out. The gentle Darwin found himself in the center of a storm. The controversy surrounded the issue of how humans fit into these theories. Darwin had avoided that issue in his book. He knew people would have trouble thinking about humans evolving from other animals.

A problem arose because some people thought Darwin's ideas were against the *Bible*. The *Bible* makes no mention of species changing or evolving. Some people still disapprove of Darwin's ideas. Despite the varied opinions, Darwin's works marked a milestone in scientific theory. He died on April 19, 1882.

Summary

Today, the name Charles Darwin brings thoughts of evolution, natural selection, and survival of the fittest. His theories still create controversy, and his work has influenced many modern sciences.

Read and Record: Place the following dates on the timeline:
(1) Charles Darwin's birth
(2) Darwin begins collecting specimens
(3) Darwin publishes *The Origin of Species*
(4) Charles Darwin's death
(5) Lamarck begins classifying insects
(6) President Carter's birth (1924)
(7) Your birth date
(8) Jean Baptiste Lamarck's death

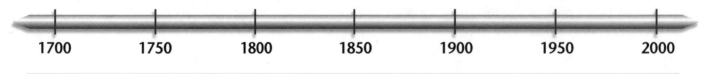

1700   1750   1800   1850   1900   1950   2000

Review: Fill in this sequence/detail chart. Cover four main stages of the scientist's life. Identify three related details for each.

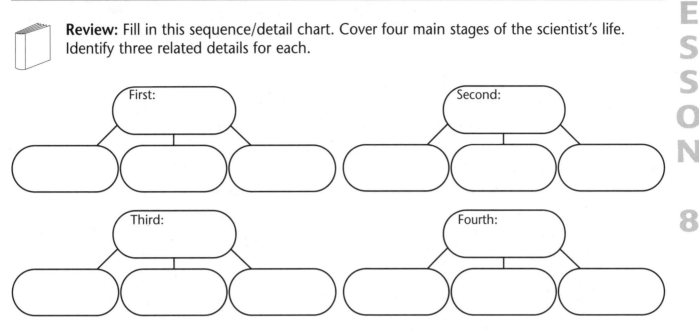

First:

Second:

Third:

Fourth:

 Rethink: Answer each of the following questions.

1. Explain what Darwin meant by evolution.

_____

_____

2. Explain the difference between survival of the fittest and natural selection.

_____

_____

React and Write: Answer this question with complete sentences.

1. What are three traits that you would like to see disappear as human beings evolve? Why?

a. _____

_____

b. _____

_____

c. _____

_____

Gregor Johann Mendel (1822–1884)

Preview: Look through the text. Find the author's subject and main topics. Do this by looking at the title of the article and the boldface headings marked A, B, C, and D. Use this information to predict the main idea of this article.

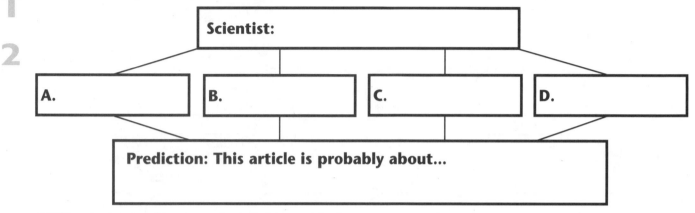

Scientist:

| A. | B. | C. | D. |

Prediction: This article is probably about...

Prepare: Match each definition with the correct word. Use the glossary if you need help.

_____ 1. member of a religious group who lives in monastery	**a.** genetics
_____ 2. characteristic	**b.** geology
_____ 3. study of heredity	**c.** trait
_____ 4. strongest	**d.** dominant
_____ 5. weakest	**e.** recessive
_____ 6. study of the history and structure of the earth	**f.** monk

Gregor Johann Mendel

Gregor Johann Mendel was an Austrian **monk** who discovered the basic laws of heredity. He founded the modern science of **genetics.** Unfortunately, Mendel received no credit for his work during his lifetime.

A. Early Life
Johann Mendel was born on July 22, 1822, in Heinzendorf, Austria. Heinzendorf was a small farming town. The farm was a poor one, but Johann learned much about nature there. In school, Johann was an excellent student. When he was 11, a schoolmaster urged his parents to send him to a higher school in a town 20 miles from home.

But Johann's family could afford to pay very little towards his education. Therefore, he received half of the food that the other students received. He was constantly hungry, weak, and ill. When he was 16, his father was seriously injured in a farm accident. Now, no help at all came from home. Even though life was very difficult for him, Johann still maintained excellent grades.

B. Order of Monks

Mendel graduated from the University of Olmutz in 1842. A physics teacher suggested that Johann join an order of monks who were teachers and scholars. Mendel decided to follow this advice.

On October 9, 1843, Mendel was accepted into the **monastery.** His shyness made being a parish priest difficult for him. He was assigned as a high school teacher. He failed the teaching exam, but was still allowed to teach. Oddly, his lowest scores were in biology and **geology.** He studied the sciences at the University of Vienna from 1851 to 1853. At that point, he returned to the monastery and was a science teacher from 1854 to 1868. During this time, he conducted the experiments that would one day make him famous.

Gregor Johann Mendel experimented with flowers. Would would happen if he crossed a red rose with a white one?

C. Monastery Garden

Mendel began experimenting with garden flowers. He tried to breed plants with different colored flowers so that he could get brighter or new colors. For example, he brushed the pollen from a blue flower against the pistil of a yellow flower.

In 1854, Mendel began an experiment with pea plants. He used large numbers of plants and studied only one **trait** at a time. He kept each generation of pea plants separate from one another.

In 1856, after growing peas for two years, Mendel began his studies. He looked at seven traits including size, shape, and color. When he studied height, for example, he planted his garden so that all tall plants were in one section and all short ones were in another.

Then he cross-**fertilized** the tall with the short plants. He tied paper bags around each flower to prevent unplanned wind-blown pollen from fertilizing the plants. Later, he collected the seeds.

When Mendel planted those seeds the next year, he found that every plant ended up tall. His conclusion was that the tall factor was so strong that it took over the plant leaving the short factor present, but hidden. He called the strong factor **dominant** and the weak one **recessive.**

The next year, Mendel planted the new seeds and let the plants fertilize themselves. Once more he was surprised. No plants were of medium height. Each plant was either tall or short. One out of every four of the new plants was short. Mendel followed this procedure for each of the seven traits that he studied. He repeated this experiment with many other kinds of plants as well as with bees. The results of his experiments were always similar.

D. Laws of Heredity

Mendel uncovered the basic laws of heredity. He discovered that each parent carries traits which combine two factors, dominant and recessive. Combinations of these traits are passed on to offspring. If either of the offspring's two factors is dominant, the child will have that dominant trait. It took years for Mendel to discover this basic principle. When he wrote a report explaining his findings in 1865, most scientists ignored his work.

Mendel died on January 6, 1884. He was mourned as a good man by those who knew him, but he remained unknown as one of the greatest biologists of the 19th century.

Summary

In 1900, several researchers conducted experiments like Mendel's and received similar results. By searching published literature, they all found Mendel's report and credited Mendel for his discoveries. Mendel had provided the foundation for a new field of science: genetics.

Read and Record: Place the following dates on the timeline:
(1) Johann Mendel's birth
(2) Mendel begins experiments
(3) Dominant/recessive findings reported
(4) Gregor Johann Mendel's death
(5) Ballpoint pen invented (1938)
(6) President Lyndon B. Johnson's birth (1908)
(7) Your birth date
(8) Darwin publishes *The Origin of Species*

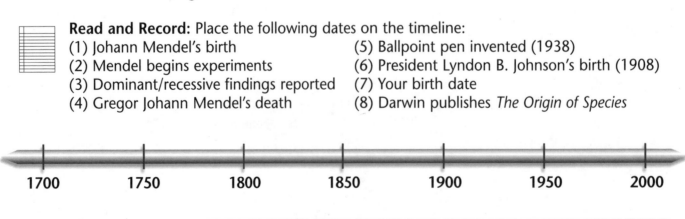

1700   1750   1800   1850   1900   1950   2000

Review: Fill in this sequence/detail chart. Cover four main stages of the scientist's life. Identify three related details for each.

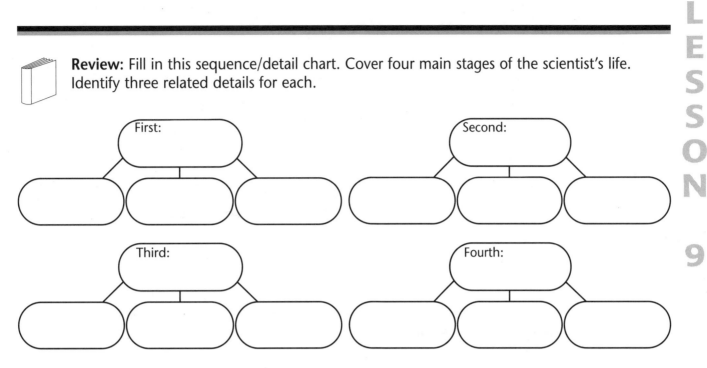

First:

Second:

Third:

Fourth:

 Rethink: Answer each of the following questions.

1. Why did Mendel need such a long time to study the pea plants?

   _____

   _____

2. Other scientists were not interested in Mendel's work. Why do you think Mendel bothered to publish a report about his work?

   _____

   _____

React and Write: Look around at your classmates. Identify one trait (hair color, eye color, height, etc.) you think is dominant. Identify one trait you think is recessive. Explain your choices.

Dominant Trait: _____ Explanation:
Recessive Trait: _____ Explanation:

Rachel Carson (1907–1964)

Preview: Look through the text. Find the author's subject and main topics. Do this by looking at the title of the article and the boldface headings marked A, B, C, and D. Use this information to predict the main idea of this article.

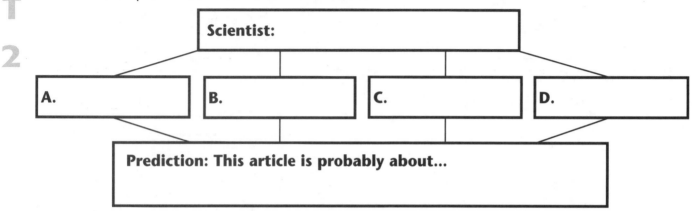

Scientist:

A.　　B.　　C.　　D.

Prediction: This article is probably about...

Prepare: Match each definition with the correct word. Use the glossary if you need help.

_____ 1. chemical used to kill insects or harmful organisms	**a.** conservation
_____ 2. study of organisms and their natural surroundings	**b.** chronicle
_____ 3. way things are connected to each other	**c.** environmental
_____ 4. having to do with our natural surroundings	**d.** interrelationship
_____ 5. record of events in the order they happened	**e.** ecology
_____ 6. careful use and protection of natural resources	**f.** pesticide

Rachel Carson

Rachel Carson was a dedicated scientist and a gifted writer. She used this combination to defend the natural world. This dedicated scientist fought the reckless use of chemicals to serve human needs. She insisted that people consider the needs of the earth. Carson awakened her whole country to the dangers of **pesticides.** She also popularized the idea of **ecology.**

A. Early Life
Rachel Carson was born on May 27, 1907, in Springdale, Pennsylvania. Her parents encouraged the little girl's love of nature on their 65 acres of woodland in a rural area just outside of Pittsburgh. Rachel grew up exploring woods and listening to beautiful songbirds. She learned that she shared the earth with her family's livestock and the forest's wilder creatures.

Rachel was a good student who displayed a gift for writing. She began writing poetry at the age of eight and sold her first story at the age of 11. She enrolled in the Pennsylvania College for Women, planning to major in English and become a writer.

B. Decision to Study Biology

In college, Rachel began well by writing for the newspaper and literary magazine. To graduate, Rachel needed a science course. She signed up for biology. Under teacher Mary Skinker, Rachel learned to look at the sea, at all of life, in a new way. She was so excited that she decided to change her major. Many of her teachers doubted the wisdom of her decision. Women were rarely hired to be scientists. Rachel persisted. She was awed as she learned about the interconnected web of life. Upon graduation, she received a scholarship to study at Johns Hopkins University. She received a master's degree in marine biology in 1932.

Rachel Carson was able to convince people of the importance of conservation and the dangers of pesticides to living things.

Rachel took a job working for the government. She wrote a series of radio scripts about fish. She began to sell articles to local newspapers. All her writing was now about science, often about the sea she loved so much. One essay was published in a popular magazine, *Atlantic.* This essay described sea creatures in relationship to their environment. Later, the essay became her first book.

C. Best-Selling Nature Writer

Carson's first book, published in 1941, was *Under the Sea Wind.* Few scientists can write well enough to make readers feel the beauty of nature. Rachel was different from most scientists. Positive reviews raved about her beautiful language. Rachel suggested that people are a part of the natural world, not separate from it, not its ruler. However, World War II interrupted sales of her book.

Carson continued to write for the government. She served as editor in chief of all the Fish and Wildlife Service publications. In the late 1940s, she again felt the urge to write about the wonders of the sea. In 1951, she published *The Sea Around Us.* She discussed the sea as the first environment and described the **interrelationship** between the sea and the air and the earth.

This book was an immediate success. Carson won several scientific and literary awards. Her first book was re-released, and both books made the best-seller lists. Carson said, "I have tried to interpret the shore in terms of that essential unity that binds life to the earth." She could now retire, spend time near her beloved sea, and write.

D. Final Fight

Carson's biggest struggle came after she was a successful **environmental** author and speaker. Even though she was dying of cancer, she was moved to action by a letter she received in 1958. A friend wrote to say that **DDT,** a popular and effective pesticide, had been sprayed near her home to control mosquitoes. The result was seven dead songbirds.

Carson worked hard at researching the use of pesticides. She was horrified by what she discovered. In trying to kill mosquitoes, sprayers were also poisoning the land and sea. Rachel gathered all her facts. Arguing for biological pest control rather than chemical control, she finished *The Silent Spring* in 1962. Supreme Court Justice William O. Douglas called the book "the most important **chronicle** of this century for the human race." This book caused debate and controversy. Eventually President Kennedy set up a commission to study the issue. Never again could chemicals be used without some investigation into their possible harmful effects.

Summary

By the time Rachel Carson died on April 14, 1964, she had testified before Congress and on television. She had won awards from leading **conservation** groups. Carson had helped Americans understand that all living things are interrelated. What is done to one living being affects the lives of others. She taught a great lesson to humanity.

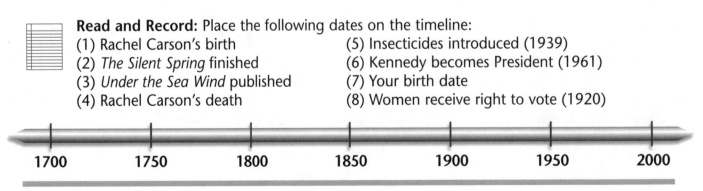

Read and Record: Place the following dates on the timeline:
(1) Rachel Carson's birth
(2) *The Silent Spring* finished
(3) *Under the Sea Wind* published
(4) Rachel Carson's death
(5) Insecticides introduced (1939)
(6) Kennedy becomes President (1961)
(7) Your birth date
(8) Women receive right to vote (1920)

1700   1750   1800   1850   1900   1950   2000

Review: Fill in this sequence/detail chart. List four main stages of the scientist's life. Identify three related details for each.

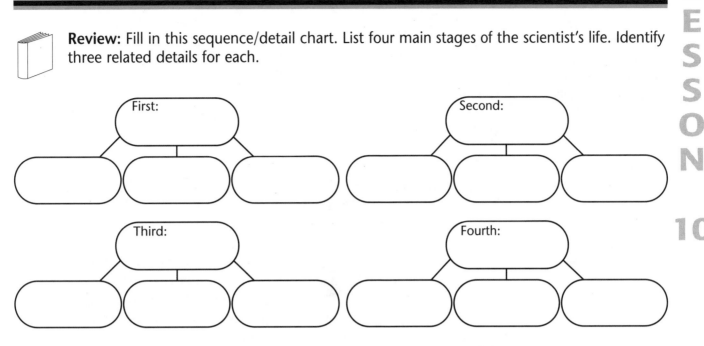

First:

Second:

Third:

Fourth:

Rethink: Answer each of the following questions.

1. In college, Rachel Carson changed her major from English to biology. Do you think this was a good idea? Explain your reasoning.

   _____

   _____

2. Why do you think *The Silent Spring* was more controversial than Carson's other books?

   _____

   _____

React and Write: Imagine that a chemical was spilled at the mouth of a river. Make a list of all the living things that might be affected by the spill.

_____

_____

_____

_____

Experiment: Counting Pistils and Stamens

Challenge
Carolus Linnaeus developed a method of classifying flowers by counting the number of stamens and pistils in each. The pistils are usually in the center with the stamen forming an outer circle. Separate the collected flowers like Dr. Linnaeus would have done.

Materials (per classroom)
Twist-ties
Index cards
A wide range of collected flowers and plants (Look for plants around your home or ask a floral shop for donations of old flowers and plants.)

Procedure
The whole class should work together to prepare the experiment. Cut index cards in thirds so each plant or flower has a card. Punch a hole in each small index card. Number the small cards from 1 to X, with X being the number of different plants and flowers in your collection. Use the twist-ties to attach an ID number to each plant or flower. Working in groups of two or three, complete the counting of stamens and pistils. Compare conclusions at the end.

Hypothesis
Pistils: Greatest number in one flower or plant _____ Average number _____
Stamens: Greatest number in one flower or plant _____ Average number _____
Will plants and flowers have greatly different counts of stamens and pistils? _____

Results
Record your results in a chart you create on a separate piece of paper. Use the headings provided below:

Plant #	Flower #	# of Stamens	# of Pistils	Plant #	Flower #	# of Stamens	# of Pistils

Conclusion
Pistils: Greatest number in one flower or plant _____ Average number _____
Stamens: Greatest number in one flower or plant _____ Average number _____
How do the numbers of stamens and pistils compare between plants and flowers?

_____

_____

_____

Doctors to the Rescue: Drawing Conclusions

In this unit, you will read about five physicians who overcame personal obstacles to achieve their dreams. Not only did they become doctors, but their medical discoveries and practices have made it possible for countless people to live. Despite discrimination against them because of religion, race, sex, or poverty, these men and women have made human life richer.

First, you will meet the doctor who made surgery safer. Next, you will read about the young doctor who discovered the secret to storing blood safely so that blood banks could be set up. Then, you will meet the heart doctor who freed babies from early death. You will also learn about the researcher whose work led to victory over a terrible disease. Finally, you will read about the brain surgeon who performs some of the most delicate operations ever attempted.

As you meet these people, you will also learn to draw conclusions. You have been working on recognizing main ideas and details. Understanding this information is a beginning. However, much of the joy of reading comes from making connections. To make these connections, you will need to make conclusions as a result of active, careful reading. The author gives you hints and clues along the way. If you recognize these clues, you will become a better reader.

For example, when you read that Rachel Carson was discouraged from majoring in biology because she was a woman, you could have drawn several conclusions. For example:

1.   Not very many women were biologists at that time.

2.   Women were told not to study in the sciences.

3.   Rachel Carson must have been very persistent and confident to ignore such advice and to become successful anyway.

Some of the questions in earlier lessons have asked you to draw conclusions. In this unit, you will be asked to draw conclusions both about the facts in the stories and beyond the information you are given.

 When you are finished with this unit, place one significant date for each doctor you learned about on this timeline.

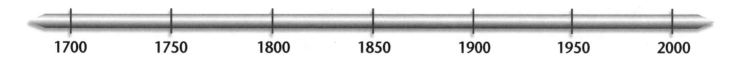

1700   1750   1800   1850   1900   1950   2000

UNIT 3

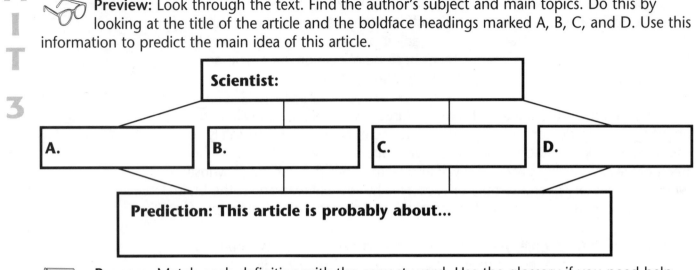

Preview: Look through the text. Find the author's subject and main topics. Do this by looking at the title of the article and the boldface headings marked A, B, C, and D. Use this information to predict the main idea of this article.

| Scientist: |
| A. | B. | C. | D. |

Prediction: This article is probably about...

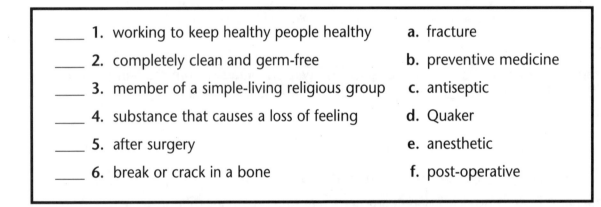

Prepare: Match each definition with the correct word. Use the glossary if you need help.

____ 1. working to keep healthy people healthy	**a.** fracture
____ 2. completely clean and germ-free	**b.** preventive medicine
____ 3. member of a simple-living religious group	**c.** antiseptic
____ 4. substance that causes a loss of feeling	**d.** Quaker
____ 5. after surgery	**e.** anesthetic
____ 6. break or crack in a bone	**f.** post-operative

Joseph Lister

Joseph Lister was a British surgeon who, like Paul Ehrlich (see Lesson 3), was interested in bacteriology. Lister was a pioneer in **preventive medicine**. He was the first doctor to introduce **antiseptic** surgery and to lower the death rate of surgical procedures. He transformed dirty and dangerous cutting into **sanitary** and scientific surgery.

A. Early Life
Joseph Lister was born on April 5, 1827, in Upton, England. His family belonged to the **Quaker** religion. Some people were prejudiced against the Quakers. Joseph and his family were sometimes discriminated against.

Joseph's father was a wine seller and also an amateur physicist. Through him, Joseph became interested in science at an early age. Young Joseph was a good student in Quaker schools. He later studied at University College in London, the only college in England that would accept Quakers at that time.

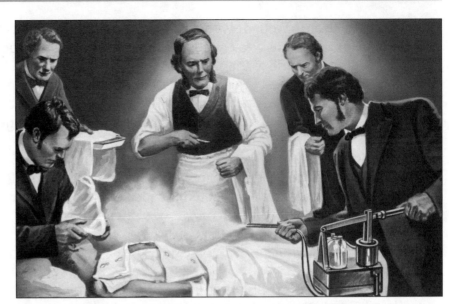

Lister insisted on antiseptic conditions in surgery. Before his time, nearly half of all surgical patients died from infections.

From the beginning of his college life, Lister was interested in surgery. He became a fellow at the Royal College of Surgeons in 1852 when he was only 25 years old. He continued to study because he felt that good surgeons needed to know all the basic sciences. Lister accepted his first surgical job in Edinburgh, Scotland.

B. Early Surgical Conditions

Surgery was a very different procedure in Lister's time than it is today. **Anesthetics** were just beginning to be used. Nearly half of all surgical patients died. The surgery usually corrected the problem it was meant to solve. After surgery, many patients died from infections. Surgeons did not wear gowns, gloves, hair nets, nor facial masks. Although they did not know it, the surgical team was spreading germs.

In 1860, Lister became Chair of Clinical Surgery at Glasgow. He was about to make one of the most important discoveries in the history of medicine. He demanded that his operating rooms be models of cleanliness and fresh air. He outlawed overcrowded conditions. He earned a reputation as a serious researcher trying to improve surgery. However, it was not until Lister heard of the research of a scientist in another field that he discovered how to cut the death rate dramatically.

C. Antiseptic Surgery

Lister was beginning to suspect that infections suffered by **post-operative** patients were being carried into the wounds by the air. Then, he heard that Louis Pasteur (see Lesson 2) was proving that decay was caused by living microbes in the air. Lister also learned that **carbolic acid** was being used to clean bacteria out of sewage pipes and fields. He decided to try to kill germs by such chemical treatment.

Lister began to cleanse wounds with a carbolic acid spray that was strong enough to kill bacteria but weak enough not to harm human tissue. He also used the solution to **sterilize** the surgical instruments and to soak bandages. Using this procedure, nine out of eleven cases of compound limb **fractures** recovered. In the past, these patients were likely to have suffered amputation and then death. His success marked the beginning of modern surgery.

D. Worldwide Success

In 1867, Lister published the results of his first set of cases to the British Medical Association. Doctors gradually accepted the idea of antiseptic surgery. When they failed to **duplicate** Lister's success, it was often because they failed to follow his careful and detailed instructions. When they could accept the idea of surgery as a science requiring such precision, their success rates rose.

Lister continued to perfect his system. He improved surgical bandages and researched bacteria. He developed the famous carbolic spray, which would become standard operating equipment for the next 20 years. He became respected worldwide. His last years were filled with honors and awards. He retired from surgery when he was in his late sixties. In 1897, he became the first doctor to be honored with the title of *Baron*. He served as president of the prestigious Royal Society. Poor health forced him to retire from scientific study at the age of 80. He died five years later on February 10, 1912.

Summary

Today, Lister's name lives on at the Lister Institute of Preventive Medicine in London, one of the finest research institutes in the world. Because of his work, patients needing surgery no longer think of themselves as victims. When Joseph Lister died, the Royal College of Surgeons wrote an **obituary** for him: "His work will last for all time; humanity will bless him evermore and his fame will be **immortal**."

Read and Record: Place the following dates on the timeline:
(1) Joseph Lister's birth
(2) Lister demands clean operating rooms
(3) Lister shares results with other doctors
(4) Joseph Lister's death
(5) First microwave oven (1948)
(6) President J.Q. Adams' death (1848)
(7) Your birth date
(8) Pasteur uses first rabies vaccine

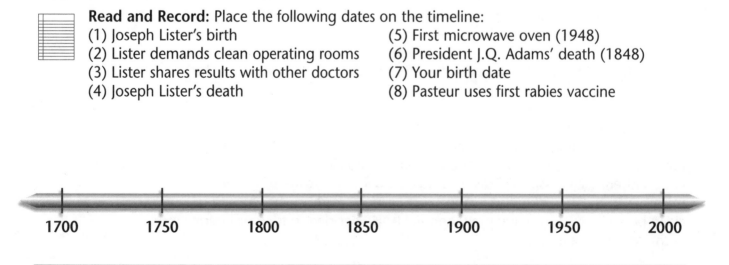

1700   1750   1800   1850   1900   1950   2000

Review: Assume you are Dr. Lister writing to a friend. Describe the most rewarding and most frustrating parts of your work. Write your letter on a separate piece of paper.

 Rethink: Answer each of the following questions.

1. Lister has been described as one of the greatest people of the 19th century. Why would he have been chosen for this honor?

_____

_____

_____

2. Although he had nothing to do with its creation, the mouthwash Listerine was named after Dr. Lister. Why do you think this was done?

_____

_____

_____

React and Write: In the space below, draw a doctor ready to perform surgery. Include special clothing or equipment the doctor may wear. List your ideas on the lines.

_____

_____

_____

_____

_____

_____

Charles Richard Drew   (1904–1950)

Preview: Look through the text. Find the author's subject and main topics. Do this by looking at the title of the article and the boldface headings marked A, B, C, and D. Use this information to predict the main idea of this article.

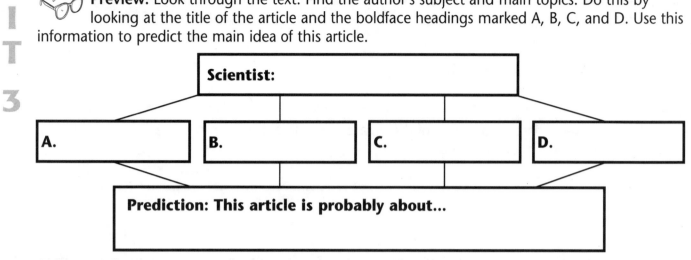

Prepare: Match each definition with the correct word. Use the glossary if you need help.

_____ **1.** saving something   **a.** denounce

_____ **2.** meets set standards   **b.** plasma

_____ **3.** group of blood with similar red blood cells   **c.** transfusion

_____ **4.** injection of whole blood or plasma into bloodstream **d.** blood type

_____ **5.** part of blood that is mostly fluids   **e.** preservation

_____ **6.** to say someone or something is wrong   **f.** accredited

Charles Richard Drew

Charles Drew was a star athlete, scholar, scientist, and surgeon. He was a pioneer in blood **preservation**. He was an American, but he was trained in Canada. In the 1920s, it was difficult for an African American student to get medical training in the United States. Drew's research and discoveries saved thousands of soldiers' lives during World War II.

A. Early Life
Charles Richard Drew was born on June 3, 1904, in Washington, D.C. He grew up in a **segregated** city where he saw few white people. He lived in a segregated neighborhood, worshiped at a segregated church, and attended segregated schools.

However, he was lucky enough to have attended Dunbar High School, which prepared more African American students for college than any other high school in the country at that time. Amherst College was one of the few schools to accept Dunbar graduates. Drew was able to study there with scholarship aid. He went on to be a great athlete and starred in football, basketball, baseball, and track.

B. Career in Medicine

Although he could have become a professional athlete, Drew decided on a medical career. After graduating from college, Drew spent two years working at Morgan State College in Baltimore, Maryland. He was a biology and chemistry instructor and director of athletics. Then he applied for medical school. Unfortunately, only two **accredited** medical schools for African Americans existed in the United States. In 1928, Drew enrolled in Canada's McGill University. He was one of the top five students when he graduated with degrees in medicine and surgery.

Charles Drew experimented with transfusing plasma, not whole blood. His guidelines were used to set up blood banks.

While studying at McGill, Drew began his blood work. At that time, scientists knew of four **blood types:** A, B, AB, and O. They knew that blood for a **transfusion** had to match the patient's blood type. A key piece of missing knowledge was how to store blood. When a patient was suddenly in need of blood, finding the right type was difficult. Many patients died on the operating table. In one emergency, Drew donated his own blood to save a surgical patient.

C. Blood Bank

After completing his training at McGill, Drew spent three years teaching at Howard University in Washington, D.C. Hoping to return to his blood research, he accepted a research fellowship at New York's Columbia-Presbyterian Medical Center in 1938. He wanted to set up a blood bank to store blood until it was needed. However, there could be no blood bank until there was a method to keep blood from spoiling.

Blood consists of **plasma** and solids (red and white cells). The red cells can cause spoilage. Drew began to experiment with separating the cells from the liquid plasma. He became director of an experimental blood bank at the hospital. He and his staff kept blood safe for up to two weeks.

Drew tried giving transfusions with plasma, not whole blood. This was a breakthrough. He got positive results because plasma does not have to be refrigerated. It is easy to store and to collect. It does not have to be typed.

In January of 1940, Drew presented his findings. His guidelines were used to set up blood banks in Europe and throughout the United States. Columbia University awarded him a Doctor of Science degree for his research. When blood was needed during World War II to save soldiers' lives, dried plasma was sent to Europe. In 1941, a national blood bank was set up for the U.S. military. Drew then became director of the first American Red Cross plasma bank.

D. Blood and Race

Months after accepting the position of director, Drew resigned in protest. The Red Cross insisted on segregating blood by the race of the donor. The army refused to accept blood from non-whites to be used for whites. Drew **denounced** the practice in a news conference.

Drew was famous because of his discoveries about the nature of blood. In addition, he helped train hundreds of African American medical students at the Howard University Medical School. In 1949, he was part of a team of three doctors chosen by the U.S. Surgeon General to tour Europe. The team suggested improvements in medical care and instruction. Sadly, Drew's brilliant career was cut short on April 1, 1950, when he was killed in a car accident.

Summary

Despite his short life, Charles Richard Drew was responsible for saving thousands of lives. Today, every minute of the day, a life is saved by a blood transfusion. Drew's work set the basis for blood preservation and transfusions.

Read and Record: Place the following dates on the timeline:
(1) Charles Richard Drew's birth   (5) Martin Luther King, Jr. begins work (1955)
(2) Plasma findings presented   (6) Bill Clinton born (1946)
(3) Drew heads Red Cross plasma bank   (7) Your birth date
(4) Charles Richard Drew's death   (8) Dominant/recessive findings reported

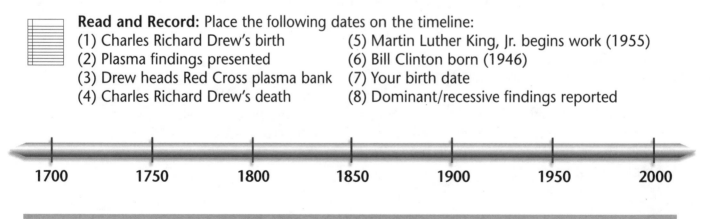

1700   1750   1800   1850   1900   1950   2000

Review: Assume you are Dr. Drew writing to a friend. Describe the most rewarding and most frustrating parts of your work. Write your letter on a separate piece of paper.

Rethink: Answer each of the following questions.

1. Drew was repeatedly a victim of prejudice. If it were not for this, how might his life and work been different?

_____

_____

_____

_____

2. Thousands of doctors did blood research during the 20th century. Why was Charles Richard Drew's picture chosen as one to be hung in the Red Cross Building?

_____

_____

_____

_____

React and Write: Compare Drew's life as a doctor to a possible life as a professional athlete. Put an X in each box that is true (doctor) or that you think would have been true (athlete).

	Spends adult life in hometown	Has hard times	Becomes wealthy	Becomes famous	Is considered great contributor to humanity
Doctor					
Athlete					

Helen Brooke Taussig (1898–1986)

Preview: Look through the text. Find the author's subject and main topics. Do this by looking at the title of the article and the boldface headings marked A, B, C, and D. Use this information to predict the main idea of this article.

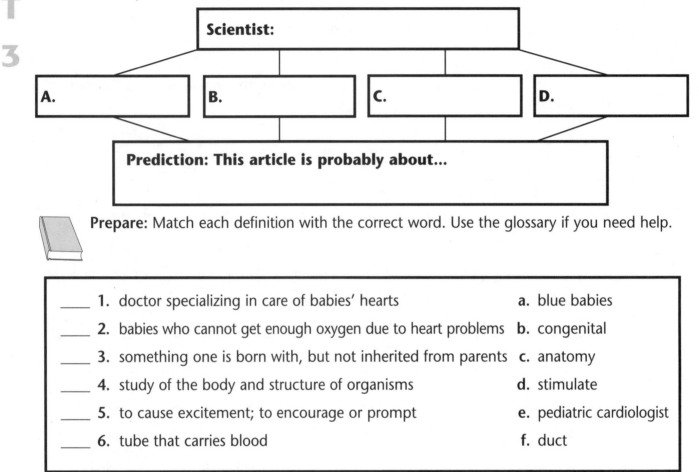

Scientist:

A.

B.

C.

D.

Prediction: This article is probably about...

Prepare: Match each definition with the correct word. Use the glossary if you need help.

_____ 1. doctor specializing in care of babies' hearts	**a.** blue babies
_____ 2. babies who cannot get enough oxygen due to heart problems	**b.** congenital
_____ 3. something one is born with, but not inherited from parents	**c.** anatomy
_____ 4. study of the body and structure of organisms	**d.** stimulate
_____ 5. to cause excitement; to encourage or prompt	**e.** pediatric cardiologist
_____ 6. tube that carries blood	**f.** duct

Helen Brooke Taussig

Helen Brooke Taussig was an American **pediatric cardiologist.** Her solution to help **blue babies** live normal lives made doctors more interested in helping to solve **congenital** problems.

A. Early Life
Helen Taussig was born on May 24, 1898, in Cambridge, Massachusetts. Even though her father was a professor of economics at Harvard University, Harvard's Medical school would not accept Helen because she was a woman. Women could study at the Harvard School of Public Health, she was told, but they could not get degrees there. She was determined to become a doctor in an age of much prejudice against female physicians.

Helen Taussig entered Radcliffe College in 1917, but she ended up getting her degree from the University of California at Berkeley. In 1923, she spent a year studying **anatomy** and doing research at Boston University. A dean gave her a cow heart to study and this **stimulated** her interest in the heart. She received her medical degree from Johns Hopkins University in 1927.

B. Blue Babies

She began an **internship** at Johns Hopkins. She ended up working in a laboratory. By 1930, she was in charge of the Children's Cardiac Unit. The great **pediatrician** Dr. Edwards A. Park told her to study congenital heart problems. She was unenthusiastic but willing. She began studying the blue baby problem.

One of Taussig's important early conclusions was that similar heart problems cause similar changes in the size and shape of the heart. She realized that heart defects were depriving the lungs of blood. The blood passing through the lungs could not get the needed oxygen. This lack of oxygen gave the skin a bluish color. She decided that the problem with blue babies had to do with the passageway from the heart. She discovered these babies had damaged **ducts** which closed off the needed supply of blood from the lungs.

Helen Taussig studied congenital heart problems in babies. She realized that a faulty duct could be corrected with surgery.

C. Partnership

Taussig saw that surgery could solve the problem. Since she was not a surgeon, Taussig could not perform the operation herself. In 1941, Dr. Alfred Blalock became the chief surgeon at Hopkins. He had performed surgery to close problem ducts in children. Taussig talked to him about building a new duct instead of closing a faulty one.

Blalock agreed. They formed a partnership that would last for 20 years. In 1944, after two years of animal experimentation, the first blue baby operation took place. The results were dramatic. The baby turned pink on the operating table. In the next five years, there would be over a thousand operations. In each case, Taussig would select suitable patients, and Blalock would operate. Blue babies could now live normal lives. In addition, the whole idea that a surgeon could correct a congenital problem took root as doctors from all over the world visited to learn from Taussig and Blalock.

D. Recognition and Thalidomide

Taussig remained at the Cardiac Clinic until 1963. She wrote *Congenital Malformations of the Heart.* She became the first woman president of the American Heart Association and also the first woman to become a full professor at the Hopkins Medical School.

Between 1959 and 1962, about 3,000 babies were born with unusual defects. These births took place mostly in Great Britain and West Germany. Many of the babies had shortened or missing limbs. Taussig learned that many researchers suspected that **thalidomide**, a sleeping pill taken by the mothers during pregnancy, caused these birth defects. In June of 1962, Taussig issued a report on thalidomide. She warned the American medical community of its dangers. This discovery interested scientists in the general study of the effects of drugs on the unborn. In 1964, President Lyndon Johnson awarded Taussig the highest civilian honor, the Medal of Freedom. She received this honor for her role in stopping the use of thalidomide.

Summary

Dr. Taussig died on May 20, 1986, as the result of a car accident. She had won worldwide fame for her work on congenital defects. Many of her former blue babies had remained in contact with her. Dr. Richard Ross, dean of the Hopkins Medical School, called her "the first lady of **cardiology** in the world." That comment represented quite an achievement for a woman whose generation thought that women had no business trying to become doctors.

Read and Record: Place the following dates on the timeline:

(1) Helen Brooke Taussig's birth   (5) First female elected to Congress (1916)
(2) First blue baby operation   (6) Lyndon B. Johnson becomes President (1963)
(3) Taussig wins Medal of Freedom   (7) Your birth date
(4) Helen Brooke Taussig's death   (8) Lister demands clean operating rooms

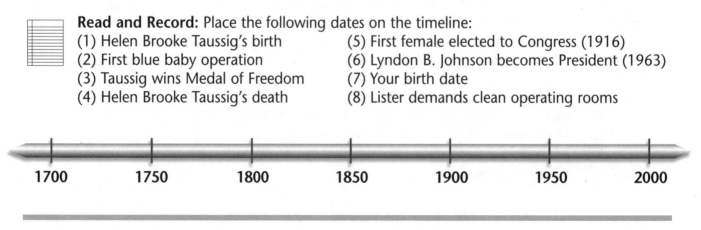

1700   1750   1800   1850   1900   1950   2000

Review: Assume you are Dr. Taussig writing to a friend. Describe the most rewarding and most frustrating parts of your work. Write your letter on a separate piece of paper.

Rethink: Answer each of the following questions.

1. Helen Brooke Taussig knew that blue babies' hearts were smaller than normal. How do you think she knew that fact?

_____

_____

_____

2. Doctors Taussig and Blalock formed a partnership. Explain the role of each person.

_____

_____

_____

 React and Write: Answer the question below with a drawing.

1. On the left, draw the heart of a healthy newborn baby. On the right, draw the heart of a blue baby. Think about the size of the hearts and the heart ducts before you begin.

Jonas E. Salk   (1914–1995)

Preview: Look through the text. Find the author's subject and main topics. Do this by looking at the title of the article and the boldface headings marked A, B, C, and D. Use this information to predict the main idea of this article.

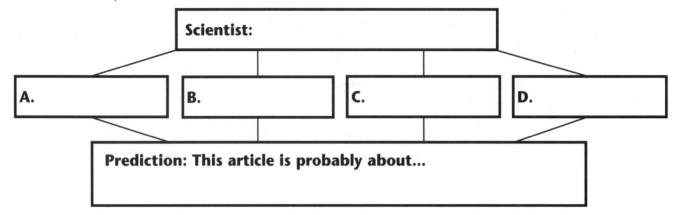

Scientist:

A.   B.   C.   D.

Prediction: This article is probably about...

Prepare: Match each definition with the correct word. Use the glossary if you need help.

____ 1. organized effort		**a.** perfectionist
____ 2. to put into operation; to start		**b.** foundation
____ 3. one who wants to do everything right		**c.** mount
____ 4. disease that paralyzes babies and young children		**d.** antibody
____ 5. substance in the blood that fights disease		**e.** polio
____ 6. group or cause that raises money to meet its goals		**f.** campaign

Jonas E. Salk

Jonas Salk was a doctor who freed millions of parents from the worry over **polio.** With the help of radio, television, and magazines, he **mounted** a **campaign** to wipe out a dreaded disease within a year.

A. Early Life

Jonas E. Salk was born in New York on October 28, 1914. As a boy, Jonas was a constant reader. He was a shy **perfectionist** and received high grades in school. When he graduated from Townsend Harris High School, a special New York City school for exceptional students, he planned to become a lawyer. However, a required freshman science course at the City College of New York changed his plans. He decided to become a medical researcher.

When Jonas graduated, his parents had to borrow money for him to attend the New York University School of Medicine. Fortunately, scholarships helped to pay for his education. He took time out to spend a year studying chemistry to help him in future research. His professors became interested in the serious young man who was so dedicated to his work. He graduated from medical school in 1939.

B. Polio

At that time polio was a cruel disease that afflicted mainly children. It caused severe leg pain after a series of flu symptoms. Some victims ended up with a limp or even paralyzed. Others had problems breathing and often died. Most cases occurred in the summer.

The seasonal aspect of the disease made summer a time of fear and anxiety for parents. During the summer Jonas was two, the polio virus attacked 40 more New York City children each day.

Salk became interested in viruses while he was a medical student working with one of

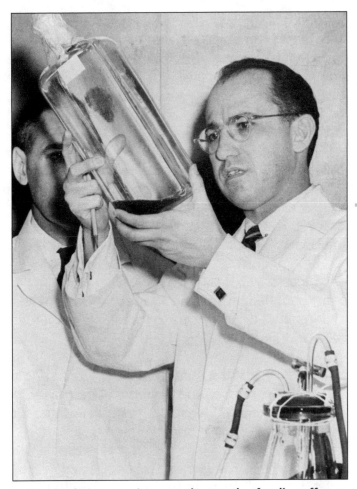

Salk's dead virus vaccine save thousands of polio sufferers from paralysis, iron lungs, and death.

his teachers, Dr. Thomas Francis, Jr. Most doctors at the time thought that only live viruses used as vaccines could produce **antibodies** to protect against a disease. Antibodies are substances in the blood which allow the body to fight off a specific disease. Dr. Francis was working on the idea that dead viruses could also stimulate antibodies to fight off diseases.

In 1942, Salk took a research position at the University of Michigan. He again worked with Dr. Francis. Salk was once asked why he chose to do research rather than make more money by seeing patients. The researcher answered, "Why did Mozart compose music?"

Salk worked with Dr. Francis on a flu vaccine for five years. Throughout that time, however, Salk was anxious to get on with his own research. In 1947, he went to the University of Pittsburgh to direct the Virus Research Laboratory. There Salk changed his focus from the flu to polio.

C. Salk Vaccine

Salk began work by classifying types of polio viruses for the National Foundation for Infantile Paralysis. This **foundation** had been set up in 1938 by President Franklin Delano Roosevelt. Roosevelt himself had been confined to a wheelchair because of polio. The work was tiring, but by 1950, Salk had classified three basic virus types. He was anxious to develop a vaccine based on a dead polio virus.

Salk became totally preoccupied with developing an effective vaccine. He worked long days. By 1953, several vaccines made from chemically killed polio viruses had positive results on monkeys. In June of that year, Salk tried the new vaccine. Four months later, when blood samples from first trials showed antibodies, he felt that the vaccine was a success.

D. Success

Salk continued his tests. In 1954, large-scale trials involving 2 million school children found the vaccine to be safe. It was declared safe for public use in April of 1955.

Within ten years, the number of polio cases in America dropped from 58,000 to 121. Salk's name became a symbol of destroying polio's power. In 1963, he became director of research at the Salk Institute for Biological Studies in La Jolla, California.

Summary

Later, Jonas Salk went to the White House to be congratulated by President Lyndon Johnson and the Surgeon General of the United States. He was awarded the Medal of Freedom. His vaccine was called "an historic triumph of preventive medicine." Salk returned home to continue his work and to search for new triumphs. Children today can be protected by swallowing the newer Sabin vaccine, but Salk remains famous as the first person to conquer polio. Salk spent his last years searching for a vaccine against AIDS. He died on June 23, 1995.

Read and Record: Place the following dates on the timeline:
(1) Jonas Salk's birth
(2) Salk begins polio research
(3) Mass polio vaccines begin
(4) Jonas Salk's death
(5) Mozart's birth (1914)
(6) FDR becomes President (1933)
(7) Your birth date
(8) First smallpox vaccination

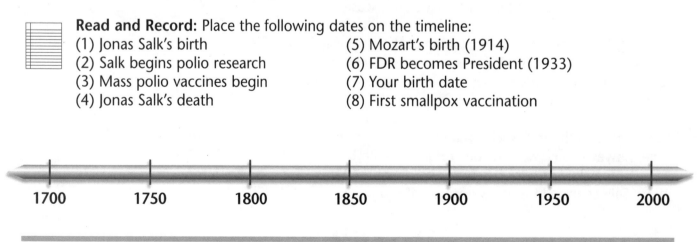

1700   1750   1800   1850   1900   1950   2000

Review: Assume you are Dr. Salk writing to a friend. Describe the most rewarding and most frustrating parts of your work. Write your letter on a separate piece of paper.

 Rethink: Answer each of the following questions.

1. When Salk was asked why he chose to do research, he responded, "Why did Mozart compose music?" What do you think he meant?

   _____

   _____

   _____

2. By the time polio was under control in the U.S., Salk's vaccine was no longer being used. Given this, why is he remembered and honored?

   _____

   _____

   _____

React and Write: Try to find a polio victim to interview. Ask adults if they know someone who had polio. Fill in the interview chart with the answers you collect.

How old were you when you got polio? _____

What do you remember about having polio? _____

_____

Do you have friends or relatives who also had polio? _____ If so, who?

_____

Have you had lasting health problems because of having had polio? _____ If so, what type of problems? _____

In the 1950s and '60s, do you remember hearing about Dr. Jonas Salk and his vaccine? _____ If so, what did you remember about it? _____

Benjamin Carson   (1951–   )

Preview: Look through the text. Find the author's subject and main topics. Do this by looking at the title of the article and the boldface headings marked A, B, C, and D. Use this information to predict the main idea of this article.

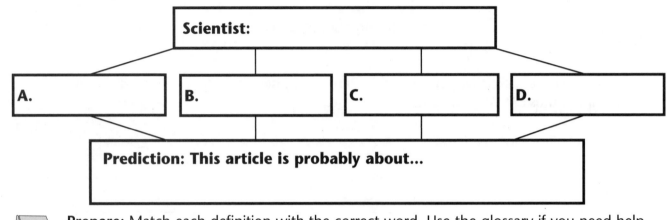

Prepare: Match each definition with the correct word. Use the glossary if you need help.

____ **1.** doctor who operates on the brain or nervous system	**a.** intern
____ **2.** surgery in which brain matter is removed	**b.** resident
____ **3.** two people born attached to each other	**c.** neurosurgeon
____ **4.** advanced medical student	**d.** seizure
____ **5.** doctor in training	**e.** conjoined twins
____ **6.** violent action of muscles that cannot be controlled	**f.** hemispherectomy

Benjamin Carson

Dr. Benjamin Carson is a pediatric **neurosurgeon.** He has saved the lives of hundreds of people through dramatic brain surgery. He is one of the few brain surgeons who will perform **hemispherectomies.** He was also one of the surgeons involved in a famous operation that successfully separated two **conjoined twins** in 1987.

A. Early Life
Benjamin Carson was born on September 18, 1951, in Detroit, Michigan. He was a bright boy, but he had a hard time controlling his temper. Ben credits his mother for helping him through his struggles.

Ben's mother, Sonya, had a profound effect upon his life. She had only a third-grade education and was a single mother. She suffered from arthritis and heart problems. Still, she taught Ben and his brother Curtis the qualities that they needed for success. She limited their television viewing. She also made them write two book reports a week, even though she was not able to read the reports herself. She believed that faith and education were the most important things in life,

As a pediatric neurosurgeon, Benjamin Carson (left) has performed delicate surgeries on children.

and she passed these beliefs on to her sons. In addition, she gave them a deep respect for themselves that could never be taken away from them.

B. Medical School

Ben was successful at Southwestern High School and on his national college tests. In 1969, he won a full academic scholarship to Yale University. He almost failed in his freshman year. He had to compete with students who had been well prepared at some of the best schools.

Carson had trouble in chemistry. The night before the final exam, he prayed: "Lord, if you really want me to be a doctor, you're going to have to work a miracle." He still talks about the dream he had that night, the dream in which he saw all the questions and answers. He passed the final and did well enough to graduate. He went on to the University of Michigan School of Medicine, graduating in 1977.

C. Early Medical Experience

After medical school, doctors continue to study as **interns** and **residents** at hospitals. Carson spent his internship and residency at Johns Hopkins Hospital. Then, he went to West Australia for a year. Few doctors were there, so he got the chance to perform surgery often. Doing brain surgery as often as three times a day sharpened his skills as a surgeon. When he returned to Hopkins to work, he was ready for some of the delicate operations that have since made him famous.

Dr. Carson soon got a reputation for being willing to take the most difficult cases. He performed hemispherectomies on young people who suffered terribly from multiple **seizures.** He removed half of their brains, but he gave them a chance for life. Once, he even operated on a baby before birth.

D. Fame as a Surgeon

Today, Benjamin Carson is Chief of Pediatric Neurosurgery at Johns Hopkins. He operates up to four days a week for as long as ten hours at a time.

Carson has a special desire to help African American teenagers with their career choices. He insists that it is easier for a young African American person to become a neurosurgeon than a rock star or a basketball hero. "Being black often makes it tough, but seldom makes things impossible," he insists.

On September 6, 1987, Dr. Carson and Dr. Mark Rogers, the coordinator of surgery, headed the team of doctors that separated Patrick and Benjamin Binder, German conjoined twins born joined at the head. Carson did the actual separating. For the first time after such an operation, both boys lived. They are now able to live separate lives.

Summary

Despite his success and fame, Carson is a humble and gentle man. He still credits religion and his mother for much of his strength. He remains in awe of the tremendous power he has. "When you take out a large part of someone's brain and hold it in your hand," he says, "it almost seems unreal...and yet you realize that this is the substance that makes a person a person."

Benjamin Carson has accomplished much. He is a private man who spends his free time with his family. In addition to home and work, Carson finds time for community service. He talks to young people to encourage them to think about their futures and to THINK BIG.

Read and Record: Place the following dates on the timeline:
(1) Benjamin Carson's birth
(2) German conjoined twins separated
(3) Carson graduates from medical school
(4) Benjamin Carson's 70th birthday
(5) First pacemaker (1952)
(6) President Carter's birth (1924)
(7) Your birth date
(8) Mass polio vaccines begin

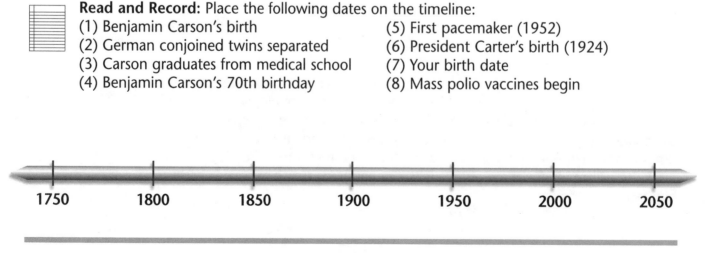

| 1750 | 1800 | 1850 | 1900 | 1950 | 2000 | 2050 |

Review: Assume you are Dr. Carson writing to a friend. Describe the most rewarding and most frustrating parts of your work. Write your letter on a separate piece of paper.

 Rethink: Answer each of the following questions.

1. Why do you think Dr. Carson spends time talking to young people about their futures?

_____

_____

_____

_____

2. Dr. Carson was only 36 years old at the time of the conjoined twins operation. Why do you think such a young doctor was asked to do such complex surgery?

_____

_____

_____

_____

React and Write: Doctor Carson tells students to THINK BIG. Study his THINK BIG philosophy and then create a piece of philosophy of your own.

Dr. Carson's THINK BIG Philosophy	Imagine you are a famous doctor. What would you want to tell teenagers? Create key words for the acronym ACHIEVE.	A _____
Talent		C _____
Honesty		H _____
Insight		I _____
Nice		E _____
Knowledge		V _____
Books		E _____
In-depth learning		
God		

Experiment: Sterilizing Equipment

Challenge

Dr. Joseph Lister developed a method of making surgery more sterile. He set out to sterilize the tools used in surgery. His method ended up sterilizing more than he had intended. Conduct this experiment to see what Dr. Lister's unexpected results were.

Materials (per classroom)

5 drinking glasses	5 cereal bowls	3' x 5' (approx.) table
5 forks	5 knives	5 spoons
5 fine-mist spray bottles full of water		old clothes

Procedure

Place the table outside, in a group shower, or in a room where water spilling and spraying is not a problem. Place the dishes and silverware on the table. Five team members dressed in old clothes each take a spray bottle. Working together, team members quickly spray all sides of the dishes and silverware.

Hypothesis

Describe the scene you expect at the end of the experiment. What will be sterile, or covered with water?

_____

_____

_____

_____

Results

Describe the actual scene at the end of the experiment. What was sterile, or covered with water?

_____

_____

_____

Conclusion

Why was it helpful that Dr. Lister ended up sterilizing more than he had intended?

_____

_____

_____

_____

Don't Forget the Animals: Critical Reading

In this unit, you will read about four scientists who combined many fields of study with zoology to advance knowledge about both humans and animals. They all made their work known to people throughout the world. Other scientists and the general public were invited to share their knowledge and enthusiasm. These four scientists are examples of people who truly love their work.

You will learn about the American painter who seemed like a failure while he lived, but whose name is recognized everywhere today. You will meet two people whose television shows have brought their work to millions. One shared the world of natural history. The other shared the world of the ocean and its inhabitants. You will learn about the "chimp-girl," the scientist who spent much of her life living in the wild jungles so that she could study chimpanzees in their natural environment.

As you read about these fascinating life scientists, you will be drawing together all the critical reading skills that you have been using throughout this text. You will continue to find main ideas, find details, be aware of sequence, and identify important facts. You will continue to draw conclusions about what you read as you look for all of the author's hints and clues. You should also find two facts to be true: (1) Your active reading has paid off. You are indeed a better reader. (2) Because you are a better reader, you are also enjoying it even more. You can now read more books with the confidence that you have learned important reading skills.

 When you are finished with this unit, place one significant date for each scientist you learned about on this timeline.

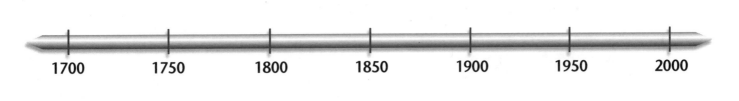

1700   1750   1800   1850   1900   1950   2000

John James Audubon   (1785–1851)

Preview: Look through the text. Find the author's subject and main topics. Do this by looking at the title of the article and the boldface headings marked A, B, C, and D. Use this information to predict the main idea of this article.

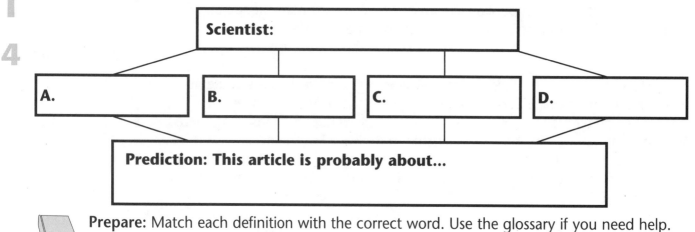

Prepare: Match each definition with the correct word. Use the glossary if you need help.

_____ **1.** scientist who studies birds	**a.** game
_____ **2.** to leave your home country to live in another country	**b.** governess
_____ **3.** to place identification markers on animals	**c.** migration
_____ **4.** moving from one place to another when the season changes	**d.** band
_____ **5.** takes care of someone else's children	**e.** emigrate
_____ **6.** animals hunted for food	**f.** ornithologist

John James Audubon

John James Audubon was an American **ornithologist.** He was one of the first people to paint American birds in a life-like manner in natural surroundings. He was also one of the earliest naturalists to speak out in favor of conservation.

A. Early Life
John James Audubon was born on April 26, 1785, in Les Cayes, Haiti. His father was a French sea captain. His mother died shortly after he was born. John then went to France to live with his half-sister and his father's wife.

From his childhood on, John was interested in natural history. He loved to wander in the woods around his home in Nantes, France.

Educated locally, he developed an early interest in music and painting. As a teenager, he studied with local painters.

B. Low Point in His Life

In 1803, Audubon **emigrated** from France to take care of his father's American property at an estate called Mill Grove near Philadelphia. There, he **banded** some birds to identify them and to study their patterns of **migration.** He discovered that the same birds who left the North in the winter returned in the spring. He also began to draw birds.

Four years after his arrival in America, Audubon opened a general store in Louisville, Kentucky, with Ferdinand Rozier. A year later, he married a neighbor, Lucy Bakewell. Unfortunately, Audubon was a poor businessman. He was more interested in birds than in his store. By 1819 he had no money and was in prison for debt.

C. American Bird Paintings

Audubon was released from jail in 1820. He got the idea of painting an individual watercolor of every bird in North America. By now, he and Lucy had

Audubon was one of the first artists to paint realistic and detailed birds. He traveled widely to create his collection of paintings.

settled into an unusual but happy marriage. She took care of the family with money she made as a **governess.** He decided to travel west on the Ohio and Missouri Rivers so that he could paint some birds. The boat captain provided him with free passage. In exchange, Audubon had to hunt for **game** to feed the crew each day.

When he returned, he made a little money by painting signs and portraits. He also gave lessons in drawing and French. He continued to work on his idea of a collection of paintings of American birds. Up to this time, artists painted birds in a very unnatural manner. They usually used stuffed birds as subjects. Audubon's birds were realistic and detailed. He painted from real life in actual surroundings. Despite the quality of his watercolors, he could not find an American publisher for his work.

D. Success in England

By 1825, Audubon had completed a set of bird paintings. He decided to take his work to England to find a publisher. Robert Havell of London agreed to publish Audubon's paintings.

From 1827 to 1838, *Birds of America* was published in 87 parts. A pay-as-you-go agreement was covered by subscriptions. This work consisted of 435 life-sized colored engravings made from his watercolors. Audubon's sons, Victor and John, worked on the project with him. Then, with the help of Scottish naturalist William MacGillivray, Audubon wrote a text called *Ornithological Biography.* This book described the habits of the birds Audubon drew. Since he actually watched the birds in their natural habitats, he had learned a great deal about them. In 1830, Audubon was honored by being named as a fellow of the Royal Society, England's organization of top scientists.

Between 1825 and 1839, Audubon traveled back and forth between the U.S. and Europe. Then, he settled down in New York. Here, at last, an illustrated and bound edition of his work was published. Next, Audubon began painting other animals of North America. John James Audubon died on January 27, 1851, in New York City.

Summary

This painter of birds, who had such a hard time making ends meet in life, has since been honored in many ways. Today, the Audubon Society is named after him. The Audubon Shrine and Wildlife Sanctuary is located today in Audubon, Pennsylvania. He was honored in the Hall of Fame for Great Americans in 1900. The type of pictures that John James Audubon painted are so common today that they no longer seem remarkable, as they did when he first painted them.

Read and Record: Place the following dates on the timeline:

(1) John James Audubon's birth (5) Texas becomes a state (1845)
(2) *Birds of America* first published (6) Lincoln becomes President (1861)
(3) Audubon honored in Hall of Fame (7) Your birth date
(4) John James Audubon's death (8) First nomenclature book published

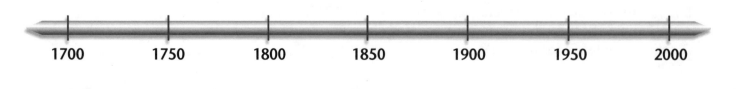

| 1700 | 1750 | 1800 | 1850 | 1900 | 1950 | 2000 |

Review: A résumé lists a person's skills, experiences, and education that make that person qualified for a job. List three things John James Audubon might include on his résumé.

Rethink: Answer each of the following questions.

1. What did Audubon do when he first came to America?

_____

_____

_____

_____

_____

_____

John James Audubon

1. Skill or talent:

2. Experience:

3. Education:

2. Why did Audubon choose to travel instead of staying home to paint?

_____

_____

_____

_____

_____

_____

React and Write: Research in a library to answer this question.

1. Find a book with some of Audubon's paintings in it. Describe the artwork you see.

_____

_____

_____

_____

David Attenborough (1926–   )

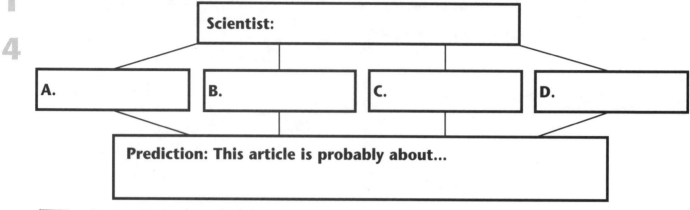

Preview: Look through the text. Find the author's subject and main topics. Do this by looking at the title of the article and the boldface headings marked A, B, C, and D. Use this information to predict the main idea of this article.

Scientist:

A.   B.   C.   D.

Prediction: This article is probably about...

Prepare: Match each definition with the correct word. Use the glossary if you need help.

_____ 1. scientist who studies animals

_____ 2. study of the beginning and development of humans

_____ 3. small salamander

_____ 4. one who takes care of or runs something

_____ 5. planned working trip

_____ 6. distant; out-of-the-way

a. newt

b. expedition

c. remote

d. zoologist

e. curator

f. anthropology

David Attenborough

David Attenborough is a British television broadcaster and producer. He is also a writer, a **zoologist,** a conservationist, and a naturalist. He has studied **anthropology** and geology. He has combined all of these skills to make natural history an exciting and fascinating story for vast audiences.

A. Early Life
David Attenborough was born on May 8, 1926, in London, England. His family valued intellectual curiosity, and David grew up exploring nature. His brother says that David spent his childhood either "under a stone or in a pond catching **newts** and tadpoles." His father encouraged him in these interests and even gave him a salamander for a seventh birthday present.

The Attenborough home was full of scientists discussing their research. David respected and **idolized** these scientists. He took this interest to school where he was a good student. In 1947, he received his degree in zoology and geology from Cambridge University.

B. The BBC

After two years in the navy, Attenborough became an editorial assistant for an educational publisher. However, this job was not very interesting for him. In 1952, he began producing television shows for the British Broadcasting Company (BBC). Attenborough and Jack Lester, **curator** of reptiles at the London Zoo, got an idea. Instead of parading zoo animals in front of the camera, why not televise animals in the wild?

In 1954, Lester and Attenborough went on the first of a series of **expeditions** to film wild animals. They traveled to West Africa and returned to produce the first *Zoo Quest*. After the first broadcast, Lester became ill. Attenborough took over duties in front of the camera. The program was quite successful and ran for the next ten years. During this time, Attenborough traveled around the world to many **remote** places.

Through his films, David Attenborough has made people aware of the beauty and greatness of the natural world and its inhabitants.

During the early 1960s, Attenborough studied anthropology at London University. Between 1965 and 1972, he held different positions at the BBC. Eventually he was the director of programs for the whole network. Despite the many filming expeditions, he grew tired of all the **administrative** demands. He decided to resign so that he could write and film projects that interested him.

C. Life on Earth

Attenborough was interested in a whole series based on natural history. He spent three years on the project. The project was funded by several sources of money. Hundreds of universities provided research and suggestions, and Attenborough finally completed *Life on Earth* in 1979.

This program was an outline of the development of life on Earth in a series of 13 television shows. Attenborough used fossils, plants, and animals to describe the evolution of the earth. He wrote the script and traveled the world to get his pictures. When he was finished, the program attracted more than ten million viewers each week. The show pleased both viewers and critics. When Attenborough turned the idea into a book, it became a Book-of-the-Month selection. It has since been translated into 18 languages.

D. The Living Planet

Life on Earth was the high point of a combination of all of Attenborough's interests. He won numerous awards for conservation and television production. He received many honorary degrees from universities. In 1984, he produced and wrote *The Living Planet,* the story of the earth's surface and its colonization by plants and animals. He added the story of lakes, volcanoes, plains, jungles, grasslands, and deserts to his picture of animal life on earth. The interrelationships of all living things gave him a chance to stress his conservationist ideas.

The Living Planet also studied the more artificial world people have created. Attenborough offered three rules for people today:

1. "We must not exploit stocks of animals and plants"
2. "We must not so grossly change the face of the earth that we interfere with the basic processes that sustain life"
3. "We must do our utmost to maintain the diversity of Earth's animals and plants..."

Summary

Attenborough set new standards for the presentation of natural history to nonscientists. Through scripts and films, David Attenborough has raised the awareness of the people in his audiences to the beauty and greatness of the natural world and its inhabitants.

Read and Record: Place the following dates on the timeline:
(1) David Attenborough's birth
(2) Attenborough publishes *Life on Earth*
(3) Attenborough finishes *The Living Planet*
(4) David Attenborough's 80th birthday
(5) San Francisco earthquake (1906)
(6) John F. Kennedy born (1917)
(7) Your birth date
(8) *Birds of America* first published

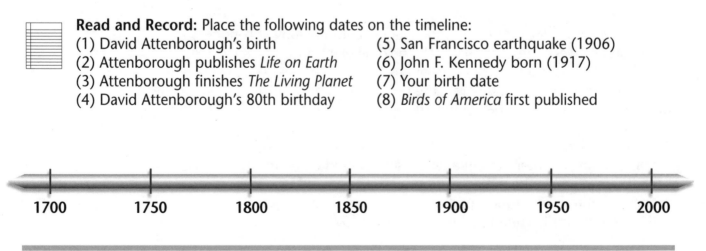

| 1700 | 1750 | 1800 | 1850 | 1900 | 1950 | 2000 |

Review: A résumé lists a person's skills, experiences, and education that make that person qualified for a job. List three things David Attenborough might include on his résumé.

Rethink: Answer each of the following questions.

1. How does Attenborough's first job relate to the works for which he became famous?

_____

_____

_____

_____

David Attenborough

1. Skill or talent:

2. Experience:

3. Education:

2. It is said that David Attenborough's gift for storytelling added a great deal to his productions. Why would storytelling skills be helpful in a factual film about animals and nature?

_____

_____

_____

_____

React and Write: Match each item below with the correct science. Write *a* for zoology, *b* for geology, or *c* for anthropology.

_____ 1. parrot	_____ 6. river	**a.** zoology
_____ 2. rocks	_____ 7. seal	**b.** geology
_____ 3. snake	_____ 8. carving tools	**c.** anthropology
_____ 4. cave paintings	_____ 9. hippo	
_____ 5. mountains	_____ 10. volcano	

Jane Goodall (1934–)

Preview: Look through the text. Find the author's subject and main topics. Do this by looking at the title of the article and the boldface headings marked A, B, C, and D. Use this information to predict the main idea of this article.

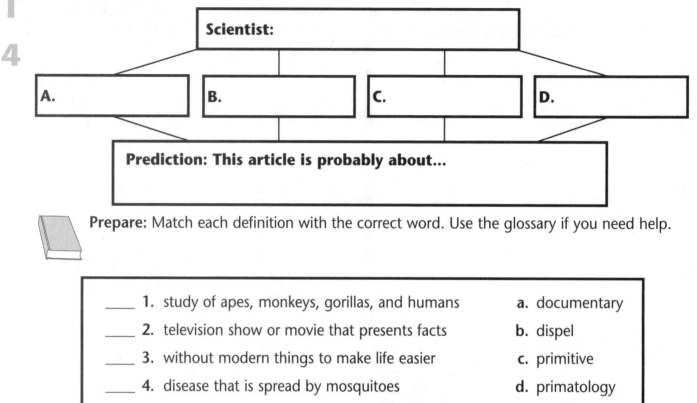

Scientist:

A.

B.

C.

D.

Prediction: This article is probably about...

Prepare: Match each definition with the correct word. Use the glossary if you need help.

_____ 1. study of apes, monkeys, gorillas, and humans   **a.** documentary

_____ 2. television show or movie that presents facts   **b.** dispel

_____ 3. without modern things to make life easier   **c.** primitive

_____ 4. disease that is spread by mosquitoes   **d.** primatology

_____ 5. to prove to be false   **e.** cannibalism

_____ 6. feeding on others of one's own kind   **f.** malaria

Jane Goodall

Jane Goodall is a zoologist who became famous after studying chimpanzees in Tanzania, Africa. She saw that animals in **captivity**—in zoos—are very different from animals in the wild, which is their natural surroundings. Her research with chimps took more than 25 years and made **primatology** popular. It represents the longest field-study of animals.

A. Early Life

Jane Goodall was born on April 3, 1934, in London, England. Raised and schooled in London and Bournemouth, she spent her childhood dreaming of going to Africa to study animals. Once she spent a whole day in a stuffy henhouse to see a hen lay eggs. Often, she went to the zoo to take notes on the various animals there.

Eighteen months after her arrival in Kenya, Goodall was able to get close to the chimps. She was to study them for years.

Jane left school at the age of 18. She worked as a secretary at Oxford University and as an assistant at a **documentary** film company. She saved her money for a trip to Africa. In 1957, her chance came when an old school friend asked her to visit Kenya. Her childhood dream had come true!

B. First Trip to Africa

Once in Africa, Jane arranged to meet Louis S. B. Leakey, the curator of the Coryndon Museum. Jane had no university training and no scientific qualifications. On **instinct,** Leakey hired her as an assistant to find fossils and study monkeys. Within a year, he suggested that Goodall study chimpanzees in the wild. Many scientists feared the dangers of both the forests and the animals, but Goodall was willing. By 1960, Leakey found funding, but there was a catch. No one was willing to finance a young girl alone in the jungle. Therefore, Jane's mother went with her.

C. Chimp-Girl

The Goodalls went to the Gombe Stream Game Preserve, which was 800 miles west of Nairobi, Kenya. Jungle heat, **primitive** conditions, frustration, and **malaria** greeted them there. The chimpanzees would not let Jane close to them. They sometimes threatened her.

One day, eight months after her arrival, Goodall was in the woods. She was surrounded by chimps who were making threatening noises. "My instincts urged me to get up and leave," she remembers. "My scientific interest, my pride, and my intuitive feeling that the whole intimidating performance was merely bluff, kept me where I was." That day represented a major breakthrough. The chimps began to accept her. She fed them bananas. She ignored their threats. Eighteen months after her arrival, she was able to get within 50 meters of the chimps. She did closer research in the next four years.

All this time and discomfort took patience and dedication. Between her observations at Gombe, Goodall traveled back and forth to Cambridge University in England. There, Leakey had arranged for her to get a degree based on her research in Africa. She married in 1964 and gave birth to a son three years later. The small family went on a three-year expedition to Africa. In 1971, Goodall wrote the bestselling *In The Shadow Of Man*. This book was the high point of her first period in the jungle and the result of a ten-year study.

D. Research Results

Goodall's research showed that chimpanzees in the wild are very different from those in captivity. She studied their complex social life, sounds, care of the young, grieving, hunting, sexuality, and communication systems. She immediately **dispelled** two myths: (1) Chimps are *not* vegetarians. They do kill for food and also enjoy meat-eating. (2) The "great gap" between human beings and other primates is *not* as great as previously believed. Primates make and use simple tools.

In The Shadow Of Man described a very loving, friendly, proud group of chimpanzees. Goodall continued studying them and published a second book 15 years later. *The Chimpanzees of Gombe* represented 25 years of research. This long period of time gave her the chance to revise some earlier conclusions. She saw the chimps' darker side: their aggression, their willingness to kill each other, even **cannibalism**. This second study balanced the first.

By the 1970s, Goodall was training students from all over the world. She also served as a visiting professor at Stanford University in California. In 1976, she set up the Jane Goodall Institute for Wildlife Research, Education, and Conservation.

Summary

Goodall has won fame and awards for her work. Her studies represent the joining together of many fields of science: zoology, ecology, psychology, and anthropology. Goodall proved that chimps are closer to humans in skeleton and brain structure than they are to gorillas. Goodall opened other scientists' minds to new possibilities.

Read and Record: Place the following dates on the timeline:
(1) Jane Goodall's birth
(2) Goodall's first trip to Africa
(3) Goodall takes her child to live in Africa
(4) Jane Goodall's 80th birthday
(5) John James Audubon dies
(6) Nixon elected President (1969)
(7) Your birth date
(8) Attenborough finishes *Life on Earth*

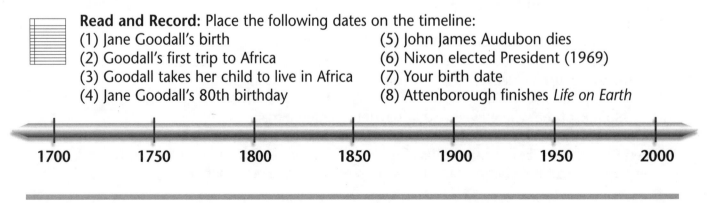

1700   1750   1800   1850   1900   1950   2000

Review: A résumé lists a person's skills, experiences, and education that make that person qualified for a job. List three things Jane Goodall might include on her résumé.

Jane Goodall

1. Skill or talent:

2. Experience:

3. Education:

Rethink: Answer each of the following questions.

1. Why do you think Goodall saw the chimps' darker side after 25 years but not after ten years?

_____

_____

_____

_____

_____

2. Identify three qualities Goodall had to have to succeed in her 25-year study.

_____

_____

_____

_____

_____

_____

React and Write: Answer this question with complete sentences.

1. How do you think Jane Goodall felt when she was surrounded by chimps in the wild? Why?

_____

_____

_____

_____

_____

Jacques Cousteau   (1910–1997)

Preview: Look through the text. Find the author's subject and main topics. Do this by looking at the title of the article and the boldface headings marked A, B, C, and D. Use this information to predict the main idea of this article.

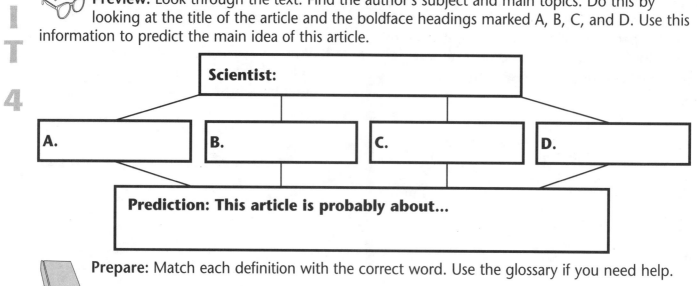

Prepare: Match each definition with the correct word. Use the glossary if you need help.

____ 1. scientist who studies underwater life	**a.** apparatus
____ 2. device that allows humans to breathe under water	**b.** marine biologist
____ 3. flying; the operation of aircraft	**c.** aviation
____ 4. self-contained underwater breathing apparatus	**d.** recuperation
____ 5. time to return to good health and strength	**e.** aqualung
____ 6. equipment or tools to aid in doing something	**f.** SCUBA

Jacques Cousteau

Jacques Cousteau, a **marine biologist,** was famous for his books, movies, and television specials on underwater life. He invented the **aqualung** that makes deep-sea exploration possible. He also directed a large sea museum and laboratory in Monaco and worked to protect the ocean from pollution.

A. Early Life
Jacques-Yves Cousteau was born on June 11, 1910, at St. Andre-de-Cubzac, France. Because his father was an international lawyer, Jacques changed schools often. From the start, he was an adventurous boy. He loved to swim, dive, work with machines, write, and take pictures. He hoped to own a movie company someday.

Cousteau's love of adventure grew. He entered France's Naval Academy at the age of 19. Throughout his early adulthood, he loved skiing, diving, racing, and **aviation**. Above all, he loved the sea. He planned to join the navy and become a pilot.

B. Change of Plans

At age 26, a serious car accident changed Cousteau's plans. The bone in his damaged left arm became infected. Doctors wanted to amputate his arm. Cousteau refused to let the doctors amputate, and he refused to use a brace. He worked hard to regain the use of his arm. To his doctors' surprise, he succeeded. Because of the injury, he never became a pilot.

Much of his **recuperation** involved swimming. For the first time in his life, he swam under water with goggles. He **marveled** at what he could see. Soon, he added rubber flippers to his feet so that he could swim faster. Cousteau's eyes were opened to the sea as a frontier for exploration. He decided to spend his life working with the underwater sea world.

With friends Philippe Taillez and Frederic Dumas, Cousteau became part of a diving team. The men excitedly shot their first movie, *Sixty Feet Down.* But they had no breathing **apparatus.** They longed to be able to stay under the water for longer periods of time.

With his research voyages and his invention of the aqualung, Cousteau opened up a whole new undersea world.

C. Aqualung

Cousteau thought about divers carrying air on their backs. He went to see Emile Gagnan, an expert on handling gases under pressure. Within a few weeks, the two came up with the first aqualung. Divers would carry tanks of pressurized air on their backs and breathe through a tube in their mouths.

In June of 1943, Cousteau tested the aqualung off the French Riviera. Self-Contained Underwater Breathing Apparatus diving, now known as **SCUBA** diving, had begun. He also devised a watertight case for his camera. Soon he was shooting and studying the sea world. He was ready to share his findings with scientists and interested onlookers everywhere.

D. Calypso

Perhaps the biggest part of Cousteau's dream became possible in 1950. A millionaire gave him money to buy the *Calypso,* an old British ship. He outfitted it as a research ship. Equipment included items such as a camera, floodlights, fish tanks, test tubes, underwater television gear, and an anti-shark cage to protect divers. Cousteau took scientists, photographers, and divers on filming trips around the world. He photographed and filmed deep-sea fish never before seen by people. On one trip, he found a sunken ship more than 2,000 years old. During his career, Cousteau's television documentaries were nominated for 40 Emmys.

While filming, Cousteau had many interesting adventures. For example, in 1955, during the making of the Academy Award-winning film *The Silent World,* the fish did not flee from the divers. The fish were unafraid because this was their first experience with people. The crew fed the fish and got them to swim before their cameras. One three-foot long **grouper** became hard to control. After being fed, this large fish followed the crew and became their pet. They named it Ulysses. He began to stay in front of the camera and not let other fish near it. To complete the movie, the crew had to jail Ulysses in the anti-shark cage.

Cousteau documented his many experiences in countless books, including *The Living Sea* (1963), *World Without Sun* (1965), and a 20-volume encyclopedia *The Ocean World of Jacques Cousteau.* In his later years, he worked to publicize and stop pollution of the seas.

Summary

About 70 percent of the earth is covered by water. Jacques Cousteau opened up this part of the world to millions of people. He let the world explore through his invention of the aqualung, explorations, photography, books, and movies. In 1963, he even spent one month 35 feet under the water in the first undersea human colony. Jacques Cousteau died on June 25, 1997.

Read and Record: Place the following dates on the timeline:
(1) Jacques Cousteau's birth
(2) Aqualung first used
(3) Cousteau fixes up the *Calypso*
(4) Jacques Cousteau's death
(5) Iron lung invented (1929)
(6) George Bush elected President (1988)
(7) Your birth date
(8) Goodall's first trip to Africa

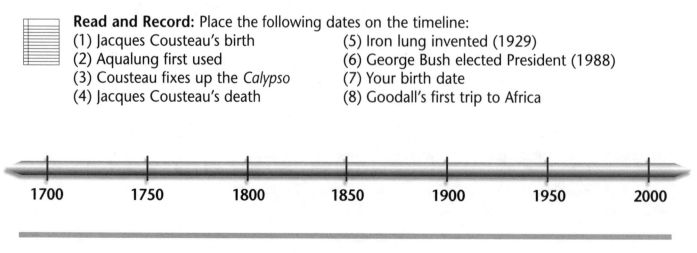

1700   1750   1800   1850   1900   1950   2000

Review: A résumé lists a person's skills, experiences, and education that make that person qualified for a job. List three things Jacques Cousteau might include on his résumé.

Rethink: Answer each of the following questions.

1. What part did fate play in Jacques Cousteau's choice of a career?

_____

_____

_____

_____

_____

Jacques Cousteau

1. Skill or talent:

2. Experience:

3. Education:

---

2. To make diving safer, today's SCUBA divers go through training to become certified. How do you think Jacques Cousteau was able to dive safely?

_____

_____

_____

_____

_____

_____

React and Write: Answer this question with a complete sentence.

1. Why was the aqualung an important invention?

_____

_____

_____

_____

_____

Experiment: Studying Air, Water, and Pressure

Challenge
While designing the aqualung, Jacques Cousteau and Emile Gagnan had to work with interactions of air, water, and pressure. Conduct this experiment to see an interesting air, water, and gas interaction.

Materials (per classroom)
quart jar   masking tape   food coloring (one color)
matches   water   science tray or cake pan
free-standing candle (3"–5" high)

Procedure
Place one inch of water in the science tray. Stand the candle in the middle of the tray. Place a few drops of food coloring in the water to make it easier to see. Light the candle. Place the jar carefully over the candle so as not to touch the candle. (Tilt the jar as you put it in place so it won't put the flame out.) Stick a piece of masking tape on the jar to mark the water level. Watch what happens as the candle burns.

Hypothesis
Describe the scene you expect at the end of the experiment. What will happen to the water level?

_____

_____

_____

Results
Describe the actual scene at the end of the experiment. What happened to the water level?

_____

_____

_____

Conclusion
Why do you think the water behaved as it did?

_____

_____

_____

End-of-Book Test

A. Write *True* or *False* for each sentence.

_____ 1. Cardiology is the study of the heart.

_____ 2. Binomial nomenclature is a system of naming plants and animals.

_____ 3. Joseph Lister performed operations on blue babies.

_____ 4. A fossil is a harmful microscopic organism that causes disease.

_____ 5. Sterilize means to make clean and germ-free.

_____ 6. Jonas Salk came up with the ideas of natural selection and survival of the fittest.

_____ 7. Invertebrates are animals with backbones.

_____ 8. Antibiotics are drugs that help prevent or treat disease.

_____ 9. Jane Goodall studied chimpanzees in the wild.

_____ 10. Preservation means to make something last longer.

B. Match each item on the left with the correct detail on the right. Write each answer on the line.

_____ 1. biology

_____ 2. theory

_____ 3. botany

_____ 4. geology

_____ 5. chemotherapy

_____ 6. genetics

_____ 7. evolution

_____ 8. immunization

_____ 9. primatology

_____ 10. transfusion

a. process of making someone able to resist disease

b. study of plant and animal life

c. use of chemicals to prevent or treat disease

d. study of heredity

e. study of the history and structure of the earth

f. idea that needs to be proved

g. study of plants

h. study of apes, monkeys, gorillas, and humans

i. injection of whole blood or plasma into the bloodstream

j. idea that life on Earth is always changing and developing

C. Circle the word or phrase that correctly completes each sentence.

1. Vaccinations were first used to treat smallpox and (polio, thalidomide, cowpox).

2. Jacques Cousteau was famous for inventing (binomial nomenclature, the aqualung, pasteurization).

3. A (newt, naturalist, cardiologist) is someone who studies nature.

4. Spontaneous generation is the idea that life grows from (living, non-living, fermented) matter.

5. Blue babies are babies born with congenital (heart, brain, pancreas) defects.

6. Animals in zoos are said to be in (captivity, chemotherapy, cardiology).

7. (Jenner, Mendel, Darwin) is famous for his work with genetics and his pea-plant experiments.

8. Benjamin Carson was a doctor who worked on (blue babies, conjoined twins, chimpanzees).

9. (Extinction, Evolution, Ecology) is the study of organisms and their natural surroundings.

10. A (newt, monk, microbe) is a tiny life form that can be seen only with a microscope.

D. Choose the correct answer. Write your answer on the line.

1. A neurosurgeon operates on the _____ .
    a. heart   **b.** brain   **c.** lungs   **d.** hands and feet

2. _____ is the study of all animals.
    a. primatology   **b.** zoology   **c.** ecology   **d.** botany

3. Joseph Lister worked to make surgery _____ .
    a. cleaner   **b.** faster   **c.** more detailed **d.** less costly

4. Louis Pasteur helped stop _____ , a fatal disease spread by animal bites.
    a. polio   **b.** diphtheria   **c.** thalidomide   **d.** rabies

5. _____ painted realistic pictures of the birds and animals of North America.
    a. Charles Darwin   **b.** Alexander Fleming **c.** Jane Goodall   **d.** John James Audubon

E. Answer the following questions with complete sentences.

1. What does a bacteriologist study?

    _____

    _____

2. What are two diseases that used to be fatal which we now have inoculations for?

    _____

    _____

3. What does it mean to sterilize something?

    _____

    _____

4. Who developed a theory of evolution that included survival of the fittest and natural selection?

    _____

    _____

5. Name one important life scientist and explain how his or her work has helped our society today.

    _____

    _____

Glossary

A

accredited—meets set standards (57)

administrative—having to do with the organization and day-to-day business of something (79)

affliction—disease (24)

amputate—to surgically remove (25)

anatomy—study of the body and structure of organisms (61)

anesthetic—substance that causes a loss of feeling (53)

anthropology—the study of the beginning and development of humans (78)

antibacterial—able to destroy bacteria (21)

antibiotic—drug made from a living substance used to prevent or treat disease (22)

antibodies—substances in the blood that fight disease (65)

antiseptic—completely clean and germ-free (52)

apparatus—equipment or tools to aid in doing something (87)

aqualung—device that allows humans to breathe under water (86)

aristocrat—member of the ruling family (34)

aviation—flying; the operation of aircraft (87)

B

bacteria—microscopic matter that causes disease (17)

bacteriologist—scientist who studies bacteria (20)

band—to place identification markers on animals (75)

binomial nomenclature—system of naming organisms developed by Carolus Linnaeus (32)

biography—story that tells about a person's life (29)

biologist—person who studies living things (8)

biology—the study of all living things, plant and animal (36)

blood type—group of blood with similar red blood cells (57)

blue babies—babies who cannot get enough oxygen due to heart problems (60)

botanist—scientist who studies plants (30)

botany—the study of plants (30)

C

campaign—an organized effort (64)

cannibalism—feeding on others of one's own kind (84)

captivity—in zoos; not in natural surroundings (82)

carbolic acid—a carbon-based substance used to kill bacteria (53)

cardiology—study of the heart (62)

chemotherapy—use of chemicals to prevent or treat disease (16)

chronicle—a record of events in the order they happened (48)

civilian—person who is not in the military; not related to the military (35)

classification—grouping into categories by shared features (31)

congenital—something one is born with, but not inherited from parents (60)

conjoined twins—two people born attached to each other (68)

conservation—careful use and protection of natural resources (48)

curator—one who takes care of or runs something (79)

D

DDT—a pesticide used to control insects, but that can harm other plants or animals (48)

denounce—to say someone or something is wrong (58)

diabetes—disease in which the body cannot use sugar (24)

diphtheria—a deadly children's disease (17)

dispel—to prove to be false (84)

documentary—a television show or movie that presents facts about a subject (83)

dominant—strongest (44)

duct—tube that carries blood (61)

duplicate—repeat with the same results as the original (54)

E

eccentric—a strange and unusual person (17)

ecology—study of organisms and their natural surroundings (46)

emigrate—to leave one's home country to live in another country (75)

environmental—having to do with our natural surroundings (48)

enzyme—substance made in living organisms that causes change (21)

epidemic—a fast-spreading outbreak of disease (9)

evolution—idea that suggests life on Earth is constantly changing and developing (34)

evolve—to change over time (39)

expedition—a planned working trip (79)

extinct—no longer living (39)

F

fatal—causing death (14)

fermentation—chemical reaction used to make wine (13)

fertilize—to join the male and female reproductive cells together (44)

fossil—remains or evidence of an animal or plant that lived long ago (9)

foundation—a group or cause that raises money to meet its goals (66)

fracture—a break or crack in a bone (54)

G

game—animals hunted for food or sport (75)

genetics—the study of heredity (42)

genus—group of similar life forms that cannot mate with each other (32)

geology—study of the history and structure of the earth (43)

germ—harmful microscopic organism that causes disease (14)

governess—woman who takes care of someone else's children (75)

grouper—a large fish that lives near the bottom of seas and oceans (88)

H

hemispherectomy—surgery in which part of the brain is removed (68)

heredity—the passing of characteristics from parents to their children (29)

I

idolize—to look up to; to have respect for (79)

immortal—undying; alive forever (54)

immune—not affected by disease (8)

immunization—process of making someone able to resist disease (10)

infection—results when viruses or bacteria invade an organism (9)

inoculation—use of diseased matter to fight disease (9)

instinct—gut feeling (83)

insulin—substance that controls blood sugar levels in the body (24)

intern—an advanced medical student (69)

internship—time of hands-on learning before getting a full-time job (61)

interrelationship—the way things are connected to each other (48)

invertebrate—animal without a backbone (34)

L

lecturer—one who gives speeches to teach people (25)

M

malaria—disease that is spread by mosquitoes (83)

marine biologist—scientist who studies underwater life (86)

marvel—to look at with awe and wonder (87)

microbe—a tiny life form that can be seen only with a microscope (10)

microbiologist—person who studies very small life forms (12)

migration—moving from one place to another when the season changes (75)

monastery—place where members of a religious group work and live (43)

monk—member of a religious group who lives in a monastery (42)

mount—to put into operation; to start (64)

N

natural history—science of studying nature (38)

natural selection—Darwin's idea that those suited to live in a certain place will survive (40)

naturalist—one who studies nature (39)

neurosurgeon—doctor who operates on the brain or nervous system (68)

newt—a small salamander (78)

O

obituary—description of a person's life written after that person dies (54)

ornithologist—scientist who studies birds (74)

P

pancreas—organ in the body that makes digestive juices (25)

pasteurization—process used to keep food germ-free (13)

pediatrician—children's doctor (61)

pediatric cardiologist—children's heart doctor (60)

penicillin—drug made from mold; used to treat disease (20)

perfectionist—one who wants to do everything exactly right (64)

pesticide—chemical used to kill insects or other harmful organisms (46)

petri dish—shallow dish with a loose-fitting cover; used in labs (21)

pistil—center part of a flower that contains a female reproductive cell (31)

plasma—part of blood that is mostly fluids (58)

polio—disease that paralyzes babies and young children (64)

pollen—yellow powder found in a flower's petal that contains male reproductive cells (31)

post-operative—after surgery (53)

preservation—saving something; making something last longer (56)

preventive medicine—working to keep healthy people healthy (52)

primatology—study of apes, monkeys, gorillas, and humans (82)

primitive—without modern things that can make life easier (83)

Q

Quaker—member of a simple-living religious group (52)

R

rabid—has rabies (14)

rabies—fatal disease spread by animal bites (14)

recessive—weakest (44)

recuperation—time to return to good health and strength (87)

remote—distant; out-of-the-way (79)

revolutionary—very different from current beliefs (38)

resident—a doctor in training (69)

ridicule—to make fun of (36)

S

sanitary—clean (52)

SCUBA—Self-Contained Underwater Breathing Apparatus (87)

segregated—set apart from the majority group (56)

seizure—violent action of muscles that cannot be controlled (70)

side-chains—cell attachments that are needed for a cell to live (17)

species—group of similar life forms that can mate with each other (32)

specimen—a sample; a small part of a larger group (32)

spontaneous generation—idea that life grows from non-living matter (13)

stamen—long stem in a flower's petal covered with pollen (31)

standardize—to control so that all are alike (17)

sterilize—to make clean and germ-free (54)

stimulate—to cause excitement; to encourage or prompt (61)

survival of the fittest—Darwin's idea that the stronger, better equipped will survive (40)

symptom—reaction or condition caused by disease (26)

syphilis—venereal disease that was deadly before 1900 (18)

T

thalidomide—a sleeping pill taken by pregnant women in the 1950s and 1960s (62)

theory—idea that needs to be proved (13)

toxin—something that is poisonous (17)

trait—characteristic or feature (43)

transfusion—injection of whole blood or plasma into the bloodstream (57)

tuberculosis (TB)—disease that affects the lungs (17)

V

vaccination—word created to describe Jenner's cowpox/smallpox inoculation; use of diseased matter to fight disease (8)

vertebrate—animal with a backbone (34)

virus—tiny organism that causes disease (8)

Z

zoologist—scientist who studies animals (78)

zoology—the study of animals (35)